A CATALOGUE OF AMERICAN ANTIQUES

A CATALOGUE OF AMERICAN ANTIQUES

SUSAN WARD

A QUINTET BOOK

Published by Apple Press Ltd.
6 Blundell Street
London N7 9BH

ISBN 1-85076-263-5

This book was designed and produced by
Quintet Publishing Limited
6 Blundell Street
London N7 9BH

Creative Director: Peter Bridgewater
Art Director: Ian Hunt
Designer: Anna Brook
Project Editor: Sally Harper
Picture Researcher: Alice Lundoff

Typeset in Great Britain by
Central Southern Typesetters, Eastbourne
Manufactured in Hong Kong by
Regent Publishing Services Limited
Printed in Hong Kong by
Kwong Fat Offset Printing Co., Ltd.

CONTENTS

INTRODUCTION 6

FURNITURE 10

CLOCKS 60

SILVER 66

OTHER METALWORK 78

GLASS 90

CERAMICS 120

TEXTILES 134

TOYS 148

WOOD-CARVING 158

FIREARMS 166

INDEX 174

INTRODUCTION

A new nation, a new style: American designers establishing their own artistic conventions.

ABOVE: *A wooden rooster, decorated with maroon paint, made in the 19th century. This piece was carved from a single thick piece of wood. (The American Museum in Britain.)*

Though a huge country, spanning almost as much as the 3,600 miles which separate it from Europe, the United States has found its design and taste, as well as its history, much influenced by developments across the Atlantic. And while distinctively American arts and crafts now form a significant proportion of the market in American artifacts, the debt owed to those of Europe still outweighs that paid to native wit and invention.

A large number of the earliest settlers were Anglo-Saxons from the merchant and farming classes. In one of the many paradoxes characterizing the colonial situation, these people, whose convictions had been rejected by the Establishment at home, became the founding fathers and mothers of the new American Establishment. It was their values which so powerfully shaped those of the nascent nation – a confused if idealistic marriage of independent spirit and respect for tradition, of pioneering ruggedness and love of the homely comforts.

In those early days, English and Continental goods were the prerogative of wealthier immigrants: those who could afford to buy or commission mirrors, dinner sets and glassware, as well as to transport them across a treacherous ocean at a time when containers and air freight were unknown. The War of Independence brought an impetus in the production of indigenous luxuries, but growth was slow in coming. Victory over the British Crown had brought freedom from British taxes and laws, but at the same time it denied liberated tradesmen and artisans the assurance of monied patronage.

The demography of the new nation changed; from a refuge for the idealist and the misfit it became a land of opportunity for the economically oppressed. Meanwhile the decorative arts concentrated on things utilitarian, until a new elite created by commerce could give them the support no longer supplied by privilege and inheritance. Then it was still to the new styles of Britain and the French Empire that the premier American craftsmen looked for their inspiration, even if they redefined the language of their art as creatively as they did the spoken language they shared with their former masters.

But the strands of design influence are not as unified as the political and social dominance of Anglo-Saxon culture might lead one to believe. French Creole in the Louisiana Territory; German in Lancaster and Bucks County, Pennsylvania; Scandinavian in the northern Midwest and Spanish in the Southwest – all these nationalities lent their particular gloss to the products of the cabinet maker, woodcarver, silversmith and other craftsmen. Usually, though not always, these other ethnic influences were felt most strongly in less sophisticated items, in pieces made for local use in communities of small farmers, rather than for the parlors of city businessmen.

Today these articles of country furnishing and folk art often command as high – or higher – prices than less inspired 'Chippendale' or 'Victorian' examples translated into American idiom from the original English. It was not until the last years of the 19th century that American designers attained the full confidence of their own aesthetic convictions. Then they began to create truly original works which have since reversed the flow of inspiration across the Atlantic, influencing the progress of European applied arts in an unmistakeable way.

As recently as fifteen to twenty years ago, American antiques were a largely unexploited field. With the exception of the great names in cabinet- and chair-making and silversmithing – confined primarily to the colonial, post-colonial and Federal periods – and the individual celebrity craftsman like Louis Comfort Tiffany or Frederick Remington, most pieces of native furniture, pottery and porcelain, silver, glassware, metalware and handicraft were undervalued and, therefore, underpriced. Fortunately for national pride and international esteem – if unfortunately for the impecunious collector – things have changed. Today, the best examples of furniture can command hundreds of thousands and even millions of dollars; a humble decoy can so turn a collector's head that he is willing to pay the equivalent of several years of an average salary simply to ensnare it for his own. Thus the proud purchaser of an A. Elmer Crowell merganser drake or a Charles "Shang" Wheeler black duck falls victim to the artistry of a master carver.

While in Europe the bias against describing as antique anything less than 100 years old is still fighting a rearguard action against liberalizing pressure, in America the concept of age as intrinsically good has never been as ingrained. Thus the term antique is used equally to describe a colonial Brewster chair, a Rookwood vase of 1893 and a Navajo necklace of 1920. The right to annex the term depends more on the quality of the piece than the years it can claim; and yesterday's collectibles are ever eager to become today's antiques. So discrimination and an eye for those objects which record important – or appealing, amusing or curious – steps on the road to American stylistic independence are important skills for the collector. The social historian, or mere lover of beautiful things, need not be so exacting. There is enough in the span and richness of American decorative arts to please everyone.

OVERLEAF: *New Hampshire life between 1700 and 1730 is shown in the Lee Room of the American Museum in Britain, at Bath.*

C H A P T E R O N E

F U R N I T U R E

From primitive sturdiness to luxurious elegance: the emergence of a distinctively American form in furniture.

ABOVE: *An early 18th-century blanket chest that stands on bracket feet. It has fielded panels decorated with geometric patterns. (Colonial Williamsburg Foundation.)*

CHAIRS

Sturdy and simple chairs, benches and stools were among the earliest furniture to be made in the American colonies. They served a multitude of purposes in the lean-tos, saltbox timber homes and stone dwellings that characterized the settlements of New England and the rest of the Northeast and middle Atlantic region.

Of the earliest 'Jacobean' styles, very few examples remain – the earliest date from about 1650 – but it is known they closely followed the English fashion of the period. Carver and Brewster chairs, named for the first governor and for the respected elder of the Plymouth colony, respectively, were both seats of honor made from the mid-1600s to the begining of the 18th century. While both were usually constructed of ash or maple, with backs and arms of turned spindles, the Brewster version is distinguished by an extra row of spindles on the back (and sometimes under the seat). Wainscot chairs – in oak or ash, plain or carved – were another popular 'best' piece of furniture, but throughout the 17th and early 18th centuries, stools and benches served more mundane uses around the fireside and table.

By the 1670s, turkey-work seats began to proliferate, their upholstery material imported at some expense from England. Less costly were rush-seated ladderback chairs, with turned posts, finials and 'mushroom' hand rests. The end of the century saw the boldly carved cane-back 'Carolingian' chair reign in the home of wealthier citizens.

William and Mary came to the English throne in 1689, but the eponymous style did not arrive in the colonies until some 10 years later. It was marked by an idiosyncratic use of Spanish and ball feet and elaborate vase-and-ring and block-and-vase turning on chairs and 'matching' tables.

Queen Anne styling appeared in England in about 1695. While the colonial avant-garde took up the new vogue as early as 1715 to 1720, it did not become the general fashion in America until the second quarter of the 18th century. The new emphasis on the 'S' curve, or 'line of beauty', meant that the cabriole leg was in evidence everywhere, particularly on chairs, which had replaced stools as the primary utilitarian form of seating. The curving leg ended in a club, pad or trifid foot, which evolved to the claw-and-ball, hairy paw or scroll foot by the 'Chippendale' period. Claw-and-ball chairs were documented in Boston as early as 1737 and Gilbert Ash (1717–85) in New York is credited with some of the finest earliest 'Chippendale' chairs, but the style did not really catch on until the late 1740s; it reached its most elaborate stage of development in Philadelphia between 1760 and 1776, under the aegis of chairmakers such as Thomas Affleck and Benjamin Randolph. Mahogany replaced walnut as the favoured wood, and the looped top rail and solid back splat of the Queen Anne style was replaced in the space of 10 years by the Cupid's bow top rail and openwork, interlaced splats with their 'Gothic' and 'Chinese' influences.

An anomaly of the mid-18th century was the American Windsor chair, certainly influenced by its English predecessor but quite distinct in its execution. The back lacked a back splat and was formed entirely of spindles locking into the top rail, while the chamfered legs sprang from near the center of the seat. This gave the piece a lighter and more vigorous quality than its Georgian counterpart. The American version had two main subdivisions: the hoop- or bow-back type, with the top rail bent into an elongated semicircle meeting the seat at each end, and the comb-back version, in which the top rail was only slightly curved, with the side rails and spindles acting as the 'teeth' of the comb. Variations of these two were legion. First produced in Philadelphia around 1725, these chairs were the most popular everyday form of seating by 1760. Even the members of the Continental Congress sat proudly upon American Windsors when they voted for 'No taxation without representation!' Their predominance continued well until the late 19th century.

For several years the War of Independence put paid to the evolution of new indigenous styles based on tastes imported from England, but by the closing years of the 18th century a new 'Federal' style emerged, encouraged by Thomas Jefferson and like-minded classicists. The term in reality encom-

ABOVE: *A William and Mary bannister back chair, probably made c 1710 by John Gaines of Ipswich, Massachusetts.*

BELOW LEFT: *A Philadelphian example of a Queen Anne walnut chair, made c 1740, with the typical shell carving and cabriole legs.*

BELOW RIGHT: *Made c 1760, this Queen Anne walnut armchair displays some of the best craftsmanship seen before American Independence.*

passed a number of divergent but sympathetic styles, including elements of 'Hepplewhite,' 'Sheraton' and, by the start of the new century, French tastes.

While satinwood was a characteristic material in both England and America during this period, birch and maple were aso used by craftsmen in the latter, adding yet another particularly American element to the design. Other elements varied according to the style; American 'Hepplewhite' is usually distinguished by its less funny rendition of a shield-, heart- or oval-shaped back, gracefully enlivened with a carving of plumes or wheat sheaves. The legs are square and tapered, ending in spade or plain feet. 'Sheraton' is much like 'Hepplewhite', although the lines are straighter, even more delicate and vertical in execution. Some excellent inlay and carving are exhibited in the best of these chairs.

The greatest American exponent of this style was Duncan Phyfe (1768–1854) of New York. He dominates the story of American style from 1790 to 1825, and his chairs and sofas are found in most American collections worthy of note. His influence overlapped that of the new Directoire and Empire styles brought back from France. Both were characterized by the dominance of saber curves in the stiles, seat rails and legs, but with the arrival of Napoleon's Empire came the preference for rosewood and heavy mahogany that took root even in the fertile republican soil of America. Noble pieces of Roman grandeur by the New York maker Charles-Honoré Lannuier (1779–1819) vie with those of Phyfe for top place in this era; the Romans themselves would have recognized the curule 'X-seat' that is almost symbolic of American Empire taste.

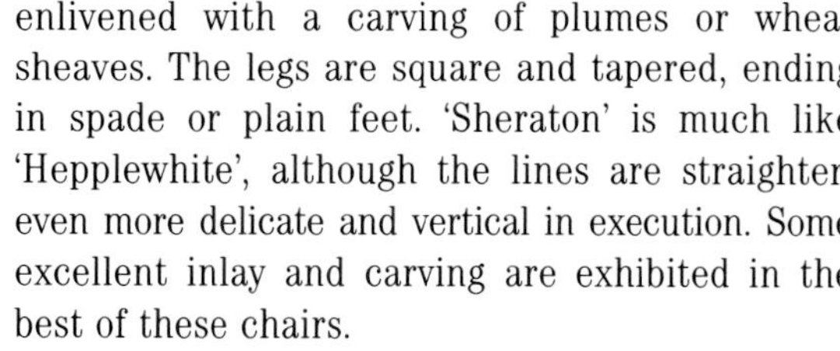

ABOVE: *A pair of sack-back Windsor chairs. (Christies, New York.)*

BELOW: *Two Sheraton side chairs with unusual half-animal front legs, made c 1810; possibly by Duncan Phyfe of New York.*

OPPOSITE: *A rosewood Victorian Renaissance revival side chair, made in New York around 1865. (Hirschl and Adler Galleries, New York.)*

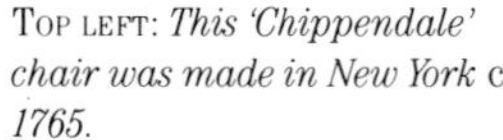

TOP LEFT: *This 'Chippendale' chair was made in New York* c *1765.*

TOP CENTER: *This Philadelphian chair from* c *1775 is by well-known maker Thomas Tufft.*

BELOW LEFT: *A transitional wing chair from* c *1780; the upholstered parts are Queen Anne styling, while the frame is 'Chippendale'.*

BELOW RIGHT: *Two Sheraton chairs made by Duncan Phyfe* c *1805 – American Regency at its best.*

TOP RIGHT: *A classic Hitchcock stencilled chair. (The American Museum in Britain, Bath.)*

CENTER RIGHT: *Federal armchair* c *1795, unusual in its Louis XVI styling, which was fashionable before the French Revolution.*

Mass-production, the inevitable corollary of industrialization, began around the 1830s. The chair was among the first items of furniture to benefit from the new wave. Lambert Hitchcock (1795–1852) established a factory making chair parts at Barkhamstead, Connecticut, in 1818, but it was not until around 1825 that he began the real process by founding not only a factory but a town, Hitchcockville, dedicated to producing complete pieces of furniture. It was a landmark in the American way of running a business, and although there was a hiccup along the way with a collapse in 1828, Hitchcock took on a partner, a former employee named Arba Alford, and was on his way to success soon after. His Boston rockers and side chairs – made of birch or maple but simulated to look like rosewood or ebony, either wood-seated or rush-bottomed, and stenciled with gilt patterns of flowers and fruit – were among the most popular types of seating from the 1830s to the 1850s.

In the years immediately before 1850, John Henry Belter (1804–63) of New York married the skills of the chairmaker and carver of the past with the techniques of the machine age. His chairs, stuffed at the back and seat, were crowned by fretted, lacy carving only made possible by the strength and pliancy of the wood laminate from which they were constructed. His interpretation of the Louis XV style set the tone that all others attempted to follow – though with markedly less success, since the competition did not possess his manufacturing secrets.

After Belter's death and the destruction of the papers detailing his process, other makers retreated to the less exuberant style dubbed 'Louis XVI'; these chairs were lighter and more vertical, their detailing finer.

Michael Thonet (1796–1871), an Austrian, had also invented a laminating process, but this was combined with steaming to produce chairs and rockers of fantastically turned and scrolled 'bentwood'. Although his invention originated in the 1830s and his furniture was made in Germany, Austria-Hungary and Poland, 85 per cent of it was being sold abroad, largely to the United States, by the mid-1870s.

American companies, too, jumped on the bandwagon. Finished with either cane or upholstered seats, these bentwood pieces – especially the rockers – became among the longest-lasting design successes in American furniture history, familiar from countless ice cream parlors and cafés as well as private homes. Certainly their popularity was bound to endure longer than the craze for buffalo horn and deer antler chairs that accompanied the push westward – and bentwood pieces were, at least, marginally more comfortable!

TOP: *These 'Chippendale' Philadelphia chairs date c 1775, and are made of mahogany with some poplar and pine.*

CENTER: *Both of these mahogany chairs were made c 1790 and are typical of the 'Hepplewhite' style.*

BELOW: *Two Federal dining chairs from around 1800, the backs of which are embellished with satinwood inlaid panels.*

FURNITURE: OVERSTUFFED CHAIRS, SETTEES AND SOFAS

ABOVE: *A mahogany and canework sofa attributed to Duncan Phyfe, made in 1810. (Metropolitan Museum of Art, New York.)*

LEFT: *A folding upholstery chair with a walnut frame made c 1876. (Margaret Woodbury Strong Museum.)*

The same tastes and tenets that governed the fashionable development of all-wood chairs and cabinet furniture held true for the upholstered chair and its more commodious relative, the sofa. But because these pieces were limited for many years to the homes of the wealthy, who could appreciate the finer points of comfort and design (as well as afford the actual objects), their history in the American colonies begins at a later date.

The upholstered easy chair made a shy entrance at the end of the 17th century, when a few pieces appeared covered in homemade needlework or turkey work imported from England. One or two 'Jacobean' sofas imported from the mother country at this time have also been cataloged. The wing-back chair in the 'Queen Anne' style, with its high back, wing-shaped protectors at head level (to guard the face from the heat of the fire) and rolled, stuffed arms, was introduced around 1720. Needlework and velvet were supplanted by upholstery in silk, damask and wool. A small number of sofas were made in the style; settees were slightly more common. These were at first distinguished from sofas by their size (in a sofa, it should be possible to recline) and the fact that, in most cases, they were made entirely in wood. Like the chairs, these pieces were all placed around the periphery of a room and moved to the center when needed.

It was only in the 'Chippendale' period, beginning in the late 1740s, that the sofa became more desirable to the increasingly affluent merchant class. Along with chair-back and Windsor settees, sometimes with as many as 10 or 12 legs and seating five to six people, several upholstered sofas with open-rolling arms survive. The seats of the settees too were now often upholstered in damask or, toward the end of the century, caned. Several richly carved Chippendale settees survive, but since the taste of the Hepplewhite and Sheraton period inclined even more toward their use, some wonderful examples of the elaborately draped, reeded and festooned formal pieces exist in collections.

As for the classic stiff-backed, horsehair sofa, many more of these had appeared by the 1760s and 1770s. Pad or claw-and-ball feet, with cabriole legs and acanthus carving or, alternatively, straight fluted legs and feet, distinguished the mahogany parts; scroll backs and rolled arms – vertically rolled if in the classic 'Chippendale' mode – the upholstered body. By the turn of the 19th century, the lines had become straighter and more severe, with a carved panel or pediment imposed upon the back of the sofa. Those pieces attributed to the earlier period of Duncan Phyfe are particularly noteworthy in this area.

With the onset of the 'Regency' or 'Empire' styles, the sofa, perhaps more than any other piece of public room furniture, assumed a massive quality. Heavily carved examples, with the wood totally framing the velvet- or brocade-upholstered seat and back, exerted their dominant personalities in reception and living rooms. Lotus and cornucopia carving weighed down the arms, while the legs often terminated in animal feet. The French influence found its greatest expression in the couch, lounge or daybed, in which one 'arm' end was raised and exaggerated to form a headrest, while the other arm scrolled either inward or outward, serving as a foot rail. The back usually terminated halfway along in a complementary scroll. The seat and back were either overstuffed in a plush manner or executed in canework.

The taste for things 'Oriental' (meaning anywhere from Egypt to China) in the 1830s and 1840s resulted in sofas whose heavy frames were distinguished by carved ornamental tassels near the bolsters, and in divans or sofas created specifically for the library, which was often designed as a suitably Oriental room. The Rococo sofa was epitomized by the naturalistic carving and buxom curves on the pieces of John Henry Belter, whose invention of a patented laminating process gave him a hitherto unknown pliability and strength in woodworking. His parlor suites – comprising a sofa, chairs, tables and sideboards – vied with his bedroom suites as the best-selling, up-market furniture of the 1850s and 1860s. This was the period of rosewood and black walnut – both heavy, lavish woods, incapable of discreetness. Other makers followed Belter's lead with lavish carving and balloon backs, but none was able to achieve his success.

TOP RIGHT: *Art Nouveau armchairs, made by Solomon Carpen Bros of Chicago around the turn of the century.*

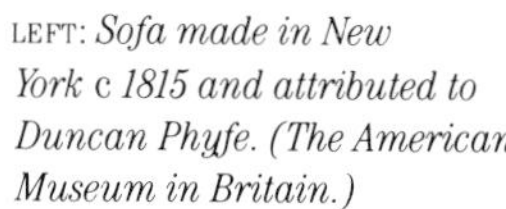

LEFT: *Sofa made in New York c 1815 and attributed to Duncan Phyfe. (The American Museum in Britain.)*

BELOW LEFT: *A Rococo revival suite in laminated rosewood, attributed to John Henry Belter and made c 1860.*

TOP LEFT: *A 'Chippendale' mahogany wing chair made in Newport, Rhode Island c 1770.*

BELOW RIGHT: *Rococo revival laminated wood love seat, made c 1860 and attributed to John Henry Belter.*

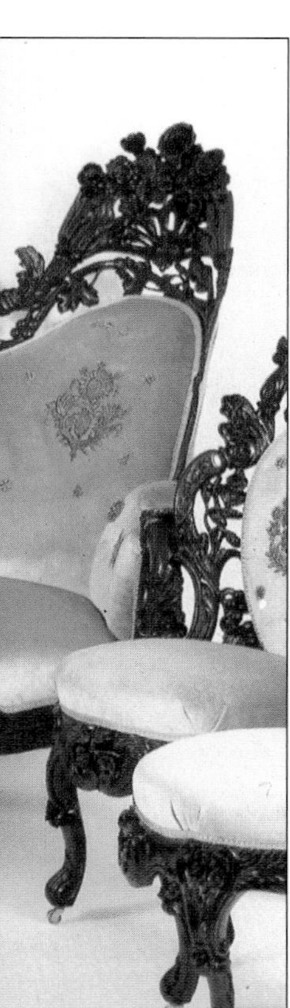

ABOVE: *Mahogany sofa attributed to Philadelphian cabinet maker Robert West, c 1825. (Ladies' Hermitage Association.)*

LEFT: *Sheraton or late Federal wing chair c 1815, made of mahogany. (Hirschl and Adler Galleries, New York.)*

FURNITURE: DINING AND OCCASIONAL TABLES

Although the earliest period of American furniture is commonly known by its English-derived nomenclature – Jacobean – many of the pieces were in fact more medieval in terms of their primitive sturdiness. Nowhere is this more apparent than in the oldest colonial tables. The largest variety, used for dining, was the trestle table, sometimes 8 feet (over 2 meters) or more in length, with a removable board secured with pegs serving as the top. Very long examples had either a third trestle midway along the table or supported the top by means of vertical supports joined to the truss.

Few of these simple large tables survive, since they were supplanted in the late 1600s by the refectory-style table, which supported the permanent top on four turned legs, either connected by four low stretchers or by three stretchers comprising an elongated 'H-frame.' The smaller version of the refectory-style table is commonly known as the tavern or taproom table, although it was generally found in private dwellings as well. The woods used were more varied than in England – oak, maple, pine and fruitwood, depending upon the part of the country in which they were made – while the skirt or frame was sometimes scrolled in a manner not found on the larger tables. An even smaller piece of furniture, but a highly useful one, was the 'stand,' its plain rectangular or round top set on four splayed or vertical legs, the support often elaborately turned. It served a variety of uses, moving with ease from bedside to hearthside, wherever it was needed.

RIGHT: *'Chippendale' mahogany card table, probably by John Goddard of Rhode Island. Made c 1765, it exemplified the transition between Queen Anne and 'Chippendale' taste.*

For dining in smaller homes, the gateleg table and its uniquely American cousin, the butterfly table – so-called because of the shape of its supporting brackets – echoed the popularity this table type enjoyed in Britain. While maple was often the choice of wood for this piece in the Northern colonies, those farther south preferred walnut almost exclusively. The leg and stretcher turnings became more elaborate as the years of the new century dawned and the arrangement of the gate, or gates, became ever more inventive.

By the William and Mary period, oak and the heavier woods had given way everywhere to a taste

ABOVE: *A 17th-century trestle table with the top made from three pine planks. It was made in New York State. (The American Museum in Britain.)*

for the more highly finished walnut. Its fine graining and the fact that it was commonly applied in veneer meant that smoother joinery was required. The gateleg continued its dominance (though now terminating in the new Spanish foot), and some older styles still hung on. Candlestands and small occasional tables began to put in an appearance, and the drawers in these and tavern tables were fitted with the new-style teardrop brass fittings, still largely imported from England.

The beginning of the second quarter of the 18th century witnessed the almost imperceptible merge of the William and Mary style into the American version of Queen Anne. The legs of tables began to gently curve out and by the 1740s had developed into the fully fledged cabriole leg, terminating in a pad or 'Dutch' foot – sometimes elaborated into the slipper, webbed or trifid variations – and later in a claw-and-ball foot. The gateleg, which had been a favorite for so long, gave way to the drop-leaf table, in which the hinged leaves were supported by swing legs. Usually two of the four legs of the table were movable, although in some of the finest pieces an extra two legs were made, so that four remained fixed and two, with shorter frame members, swung out. When open, the tables could be either square, rectangular, round or oval. Walnut was still considered the most desirable wood, although toward the end of the period mahogany, so beloved of the Chippendale school, entered the field.

The candlestand, too, had undergone a sea change. The once plain tripod base now sported cabriole legs and the supporting column a turned baluster. With the growing popularity of tea came a table designed specifically for its use: rectangular, with a raised rim or 'tray' top, an elegantly scrolled frame and graceful cabriole legs. These early tea tables, sometimes known as 'Dutch tray' tables, are among the most beautiful and highly regarded pieces of classical American furniture.

Although America was slower than England to respond to the powerful influences of Chippendale, several elements that would characterize the style at its height were already making themselves felt in the 1750s. The cabriole leg had established itself as a staple of colonial design, while the flourishing trade with the West Indies offered exotic mahogany as a replacement for domestic walnut. The flowering of the American Chippendale style would eminently suit the unique qualities of the opulent reddish-brown wood.

The types of tables popular in the 1750s to 1780s did not really change; it is the *style* that distinguishes these wonderful pieces. Philadelphia reigned supreme in colonial cabinetmaking, with Newport, Rhode Island, providing highly respectable competition. The card tables and tea tables produced by their makers echoed the elegant lines of their chairs and case pieces, although the tea table had changed considerably in appearance. After 1740, the preferred shape of the tea table was round (overall it resembled a large candlestand), with tripod legs ending in claw-and-ball feet, the support reeded or the baluster elaborately carved, and the top finished by a pie-crust or shell-and-scroll edge. Larger versions were used as breakfast tables, and the entire type is often now known generically as a tip-and-turn table, after the bird-cage mechanism that allowed the top to fold flat against the support, thus enabling the table to be pushed against a wall when not in use.

The drop-leaf dining table continued to be in vogue, with the square shape exerting more popular appeal. A variation on this was the new occasional piece known as a Pembroke table – a style imported from England – with short leaves and a wide central section sheltering a small drawer. The fashion for

RIGHT: *This remarkable Federal dining table is nearly 17ft (5.2m) long and 5ft (1.5m) wide. The six mahogany and four poplar leaves have an accordion action. Made in Philadelphia c 1805.*

FACING PAGE, TOP RIGHT: *Drum table, made in Baltimore 1810–20. Its single drawer is fitted with compartments. (Christie's, New York.)*

FACING PAGE, TOP LEFT: *An elegant Federal work table, attributed to Massachusetts cabinet makers John and Thomas Seymour. Made of mahogany, bird's-eye maple and flame birch. Made in Philadelphia c 1805.*

FACING PAGE, BELOW LEFT: *A somber Federal mahogany pembroke table. Made c 1790, probably by John Townsend of Newport, Rhode Island.*

FACING PAGE, BELOW RIGHT: *A generously proportioned 'Chippendale' dining table, probably made in Philadelphia c 1770.*

tea- and coffee-drinking and entertaining at home encouraged the proliferation of gaming tables with fold-over tops, whose surfaces were punctuated by rounded or dished corners and lined with baize.

As the styles known as 'Hepplewhite' and 'Sheraton' evolved from American 'Chippendale,' the lines of leg and frame grew slim and yet more vertical, losing the distinctive 'S' curve and deep carving so beloved of the earlier taste. The new fashion coincided with the founding of the new republic, and the classical echoes so dominant in Hepplewhite and Sheraton design found quick favor with the patriots who saw themselves as the inheritors of the noble Romans. While Philadelphia had been the capital of the Rococo Chippendale style, Baltimore came to the fore as the leading exponent of classicism, its furniture makers excelling in the contrasting inlays of holly, harewood, satinwood and amboyna that enriched tables, sideboards and secretaries.

A particular introduction of the period was the two- or three-part extension table, made from a combination of single and/or double drop-leaf tables, designed to be used together. The arrangement allowed the sections to be used in any combination convenient to the host, but unfortunately the disposition of the numerous legs did not make for the same convenience to the guests. Examples occur in both the Hepplewhite and Sheraton styles, the latter showing the characteristic reeding on the legs. While the very occasional pedestal version with sections may have been made in America between 1750 and 1790, the majority of these pieces are thought to have been imported from England.

On all tables dating from 1790 to 1820, the legs are an important key to the dominant style, since Americans were never purists. While Hepplewhite

sympathies are readily apparent in the square tapered legs – often with line inlay – ending in square feet, round legs, carved with reeding and fluting, betray the influence of Sheraton. Although the wind from France blew over the Directoire style that reached its American apogee in the work of Duncan Phyfe, French influence on table design was most marked by the appearance in America of what was up to then the typically English mahogany pedestal dining table with insertable leaves, usually having two to three pedestals, each with three or four splayed legs terminating in brass casters. Some of the largest tables, 14 to 18 ft (4 to 5.5 m) long had four pedestal supports, with the central two having two parallel legs each and the two outer supports, three legs each. Some smaller tables did show more of the Phyfe style: These include sofa and side tables with exquisite inlay and a well-judged inclusion of lyre supports, far removed from some of the heavier attempts that would follow in the next decades.

LEFT: *A 'Chippendale' mixing table, c 1765. The contrast between the harmonious curves of the walnut stand and patterned marble top of this table is striking.*

BELOW LEFT: *This Federal dining table, c 1805, has a hinged section in the middle which can be used as a separate table. The whole table stretches to almost 14ft (1.7m) in length.*

BELOW CENTER: *A Federal cherry wood candlestand, made specifically to hold candelabra or candlesticks. The small drawer accommodates tinder boxes and wax tapers. Made c 1785.*

BELOW RIGHT: *An American Queen Anne tray-top table, c 1760, made of smooth-grained cherry wood.*

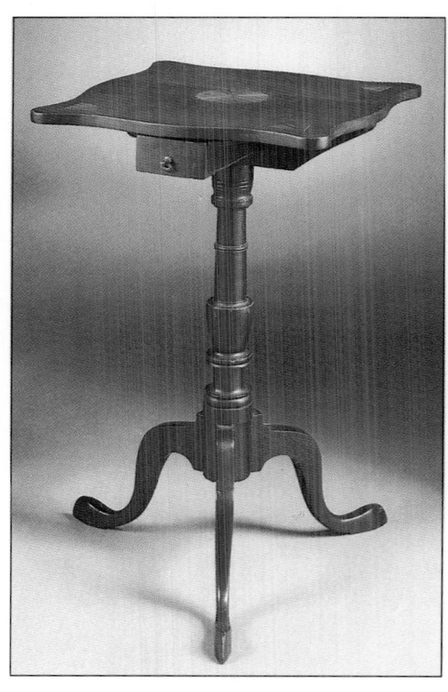

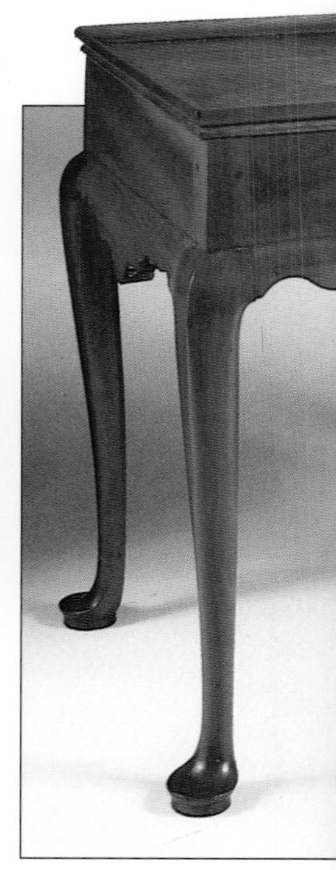

ABOVE LEFT: *The general construction of this cherry wood 'Chippendale' card table (c 1790) is closely based on a model popular from the 1770s and 1780s in England.*

ABOVE RIGHT: *A fine mahogany serpentine-fronted Federal serving table. Probably made in Salem, Massachusetts by Samuel McIntire.*

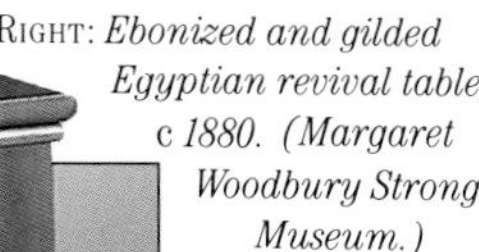

RIGHT: *Ebonized and gilded Egyptian revival table c 1880. (Margaret Woodbury Strong Museum.)*

By 1820 to 1830 and the arrival of the full-blown Empire style, the dining table had become a massive piece. The central column of the pedestal was replaced by elongated and highly carved scroll columns supporting the top, while the feet below the flattened base were unmistakably animal, belonging to some huge-pawed lion or mythical beast. Gilding was opulent and sometimes indiscriminate, while redder mahogany and distinctively grained rosewood were used for theatrical effect. Pier tables boasted marble columns and tops, and the animal theme might be continued even further with swan or dolphin supports.

After 1830, the rise of industrialism and a proliferation of furniture companies meant that eclecticism ruled the day. As in England, dining tables were made ever more massive and of ever darker mahogany, and large numbers and types of occasional tables were available in a variety of woods, from ebony in the 1830s to bamboo in the 1880s. Egyptian and 'Oriental' side tables gave way to those in the style of Louis XVI; in the 1850s French names dominated New York furniture companies. Interest in things Near Eastern returned again with the Philadelphia Centennial Exposition in 1876, which featured entire rooms decorated in the 'Moroccan' taste and centered around small 'smoking' tables.

The American edition of Charles Lock Eastlake's book *Hints on Household Taste*, published in 1872, found an eager audience among designers in the

United States. A reaction against veneers and consequent experiments in oak and other solid native woods resulted, reaching some happy conclusions in the architecture of the table. But even more striking examples of the new thinking would follow in the work of the Chicago and Prairie schools.

FURNITURE: LOWBOYS, HIGHBOYS AND CHESTS OF DRAWERS

ABOVE LEFT: *'Chippendale' tea table made of mahogany, the favoured wood in England at the time. New England c 1765.*

ABOVE RIGHT: *Round 'Chippendale' tea table typical of Philadelphian manufacture, made c 1760. The tilting top is operated by a mechanism just visible at the top of the column support.*

Unlike anything English in either form or expression, the highboy nonetheless evolved from the chests of drawers that had been made from the late 1600s in Massachusetts and Connecticut, as well as across the Atlantic. These chests of drawers were themselves an elaboration of the earlier 'blanket' or 'hope' chests that occurred in several forms throughout the Northern colonies. But the fluid lines of the masterpieces produced at the height of the highboy's reign hardly seem related to these first specimens of the cabinetmaker's art.

The earliest known example of a true chest of drawers is that held in the Winterthur Museum in Delaware, carved with the date 1678 and the initials J (I), M and S – for John and Mary Stamford, for whom it was probably made as a wedding gift. Elaborately carved and painted, with the drawers of each tier different, the chest is a unique item, strangely Germanic and Renaissance in feeling. A few pre-1700 examples exist in collections, practically all of them in oak and raised on plain or ball feet. Their close kinship to the earlier Hadley and Connecticut chests can be seen in their usually geometric panels and frame construction.

By the turn of the 18th century, pine and walnut had begun to be used in chests of drawers, but their utilitarian solidity was soon to be supplanted by the emergence of the fanciful chest-on-stand. In such a piece, legginess gave height and airiness, while walnut, ash and maple burl veneers, as well as the new art of japanning, enabled the cabinetmaker to amply demonstrate his skills. Ostensibly the design would facilitate access to drawers at the bottom of the chest, until now uncomfortably near floor level. But since the upper end of the chest-on-stand – or 'highboy' as it would come to be known – became immediately out of reach to the average colonist, that argument seems inadequate.

In any case, the new fashion took off, and the tall piece was joined by a companion of shorter dimensions that later was called the 'lowboy.' In

RIGHT: *Queen Anne flat-topped highboy with walnut and burl walnut veneer, made in Massachusetts c 1730–50. (Robert O. Stuart.)*

FACING PAGE: *'Chippendale' secretarial desk and cabinet, made of mahogany, c 1760. (C. L. Prickett Antiques.)*

their early William and Mary forms, both had six (or, less frequently, four) turned legs – in spindle, ball-and-cone or inverted-cup shape – which were connected by curved stretchers and terminated in ball feet. Both seem to have seen versatile service in many parts of the house, from main rooms to bedrooms to dining rooms; the slate top that distinguishes several lowboys from this period suggests they may have been designed with hot and/or wet utensils in mind.

The happiest years for the lovely highboy were during the reign of Queen Anne. The 'line of beauty,' or 'S' curve that marked this rich design era ideally suited the piece's proportions, and cabinetmakers had reached new heights in their craft, creating ever more handsome examples. The usual six legs were superseded by four cabriole legs, with the remnants of the lost appendages preserved as turned pendent knops on the apron of the piece. The highboy and lowboy were the delight of the New World cabinetmaker, proving that he could transform mundane English forms into something uniquely his own. Walnut began to give way to mahogany, which would remain society's favorite wood until the Federal period (although for certain important Philadelphia highboys, even during the Chippendale period, walnut continued to be used). Japanning also remained in vogue up to the 1760s, the casework often being lacquered in lavish red, black and gold hues.

As the years moved toward the period designated as Chippendale, the flow and curve of apron and pediment became more fluid. The breakfront top was more scrolled, with a central carved crest or finial and corner flame carvings; the apron contained the requisite carved shell; the sides, sometimes columnar, were carved with frets or vines; and the now flaring cabriole leg almost always ended in a claw-and-ball foot. Philadelphia became the undisputed capital of lowboys and highboys, with makers like William Savery (1721–87), Thomas Affleck, Thomas Tufft (*d*1793) and John Folwell (*fl*1775) among the notable makers. An interesting loner was Jonathan Gostelowe, most of whose labeled pieces are chests of drawers.

Philadelphia's close rival was Newport, whose Townsend-Goddard family dominated the cabinetmaker's craft there for an unprecedented 20 generations. Examples from this school are characteristically more restrained, often having a closed 'bonnet' top and slimmer cabriole legs. The Boston/Salem area, too, had its classic interpreters, and New Hampshire boasted Samuel Dunlap II (1751–1830), whose maple highboys elevated New England's native wood to new heights.

But few highboys were made in New York – where its place seems to have been taken by the monumental chest-on-chest – and none in the rich states of Virginia and Kentucky. The chest-on-chest had a short but vibrant life, spanning some 50 years during the height of the Chippendale phase. Massachusetts and New York were its home states (although some were also made in Philadelphia) and its chief exponent was Samuel McIntire (1757–1811) of Salem. Although some excellent examples were produced at the beginning of the 19th century, in a few more years it was no longer in fashion.

Most experts agree the single finest example of an American highboy is the glorious Van Pelt highboy in the Winterthur Museum, carved in lush Cuban mahogany in Philadelphia between 1765 and 1780. Although other highboys have since exceeded its 1929 record price, there is little doubt that if it came onto the market today it would knock the present record-holder, at $418,000 (reached at Sotheby's on October 25, 1986) off its pedestal.

Like the chest-on-chest, highboys and lowboys faded into the background with the arrival of the Hepplewhite and Sheraton styles. Their cleaner, more 'feminine' attitudes lent themselves better to the chest of drawers, which now came more into fashion. Bow and serpentine fronts relieved the otherwise vertical lines, while scroll, French or reeded feet set off the bottom. Matched veneers and stringing made use of maple, satinwood and other figured woods; the graining of fine wood was given paramount exposure.

The Empire style, with its emphasis on heaviness and use of dark woods, was particularly suited to cabinet pieces like chests of drawers, which could also cope with the overtly extravagant decorative elements. By the 1830s, Continental taste had infiltrated so far into American cabinetmaking that until the late 1860s, tastes as wildly diverse as neo-Gothic, Greek Revival, French Antique and neo-Baroque reached from New England and the Atlantic seaboard all the way down to New Orleans, where they found expression in some of the richest neo-Rococo pieces to come out of 'Victorian' America. By this time the chest of drawers was definitely a bedroom piece. As such it was produced as part of a bedroom suite, its form and decoration governed by that of the other members (a convention that persists with manufacturers until this day).

FURNITURE: DESKS, SECRETARIES AND BOOKCASES

In the beginning was the table, which was what the earliest and most rugged of the colonists was reduced to using for writing, unless he happened to be the proud possessor of a writing box. The

RIGHT: *'Chippendale' mahogany kneehole desk, made by John Townsend of Newport, Rhode Island c 1760.*

CENTER RIGHT: *A William and Mary slant front desk c 1710–25.*

BELOW RIGHT: *This unusual 'Chippendale' walnut slope front desk has a dummy drawer at the top disguising a hidden storage space. Inlaid with the name Abraham Grof and the date 1779.*

FACING PAGE, TOP: *Pennsylvanian lowboy, c 1730. The top drawer is faced to give the appearance of three drawers, making the piece look like the usual five-drawer highboy. (The American Museum in Britain.)*

FACING PAGE, BELOW: *A broken-bonnet-topped highboy. (Wayne Pratt and Company.)*

earliest desks *per se* appeared in the later 17th century, in the form of the writing stand or desk-on-frame, a crude piece made from oak, maple or pine. Toward the end of the century fashion declared its place be taken by the oak slant-top or fall-front desk, though the desk-on-stand continued to be made in the first quarter of the 18th century.

By 1720, when the William and Mary style was still in vogue in the colonies, the slant-top desk had become more sophisticated and various woods were used in its making. A fine country example might have a straight-grain maple top, sides of curly maple and a front of burl maple, with string borders of walnut and walnut feet. The interior of the writing desk, including the pigeonholes and small drawers, might be cherry and the drawers yellow pine. It was about this time that a top cupboard section began to be imposed on the desk, to form a secretary or bureau-bookcase.

These secretaries were executed in maple, walnut and the newly popular mahogany, and were aptly suited to development during the succeeding Queen Anne period. This period saw the emergence of the cabinetmaker as a member of a well-regarded trade, now looked upon as a craftsman, not as a mere jack-of-all-trades. The preoccupation with architectural details of pilaster and cornice, with the ideals of Palladio and the classicists, and with the interior wood paneling that distinguished the finest houses was echoed in the flowing lines and fine arched paneling characteristic of the tall secretary-cupboards. This pleasure in wood-paneled doors carried into the Chippendale period (unlike in England, where glass-lit doors were the fashion).

By 1750, the first examples of American Rococo – usually called 'Chippendale,' although the master's book was not published until 1754 – were emerging from the fashionable suppliers in Philadelphia and New York, and by 1760 Boston and Newport were following suit. During this period these elegant case pieces came into their own, and the finest Santo Domingo mahogany replaced walnut for good and all. But while the Philadelphia, Boston and New York desks and secretaries were following the 'Chippendale' mode as expressed in the closely related highboy and chest-on-chest – with fluted pilasters, classical capitals and carving, and broken pediments and bonnet tops – something different was happening in Rhode Island and Connecticut. The vigorous forms of Queen Anne were still alive there and were effortlessly integrated into the new style. The wonderfully simple yet majestic blockfront desks, secretaries and chests of drawers made by men like Benjamin Burnham, John Goddard (1723/24–85) and the Townsends have become as distinctive an 'Americanism' as the highboy. It was in such large pieces that the blocking was seen to

RIGHT: *A fairly sophisticated walnut version of the slope-front desk mounted on a lowboy, found in the American colonies from the early 1700s.*

its best advantage, crowned with exquisite intaglio shells on the lower pediment or on the paneled doors themselves.

Although the blockfront is perhaps the most extolled version of the bookcase-secretary, some of the others are as visually satisfying – plainer, with straight, proud lines along the wide drawers and slant front. A rare type, known as the *bombé* or kettle-shaped base form, was made only in Boston.

In the late 18th century glass was introduced into the Sheraton- or Federal-style secretary. The base was usually straight-fronted, with either a series of drawers below or a kneehole accompanied by two levels of cupboards. Sometimes the front would show a slight serpentine curve, called an oxbow. Such secretaries were surmounted by plain, squared-off pediments or, later, scroll tops with wood or brass finials. The usual woods were mahogany or maple, either plainly grained or ornately figured. The straight Sheraton foot evolved into a French or bracket foot when a Directoire or Empire style was intimated.

A few massive bookcases, containing a veritable catalog of drawers and doors, were made around

ABOVE AND FACING PAGE, TOP: *Wooton's Patent desk c 1890–1900, shown here both closed to display the rich ornament and open to reveal the complexity of the storage compartments.*

RIGHT: *Queen Anne maple desk-and-bookcase c 1740, with compartmented shelves and pigeonholes behind the panelled doors of the upper section.*

Baltimore, the new home of the Sheraton and Directoire styles. Unbelievably, a number of these mammoth pieces were still shipped from England at great expense. The *verre églomisé* technique – glass decorated on the back and generally depicting classical subjects and arabesques – was not uncommon during this period.

The Gothic Revival in the 1830s and 1840s supplied spectacular examples of large bookcases, so architectural in feeling that they almost seem part of a building. In fact, some of the best pieces were designed by architects for use in specific buildings. The characteristic feature of the style was the pointed arch, used with incised or pierced spandrels and raised molding. Later, the Renaissance style initiated at the New York Exhibition of 1853 was used to great effect on these large case pieces. The bold moldings, raised and shaped panels, and applied carving of garlands and medallions suited the library pieces much better than they did almost any other form of household furniture. These were pieces for the rich, who occupied the mansions large enough to accommodate them.

FACING PAGE: *A bonnet-topped chest on chest. (Taylor B. Williams Antiques, Chicago, Illinois.)*

BELOW RIGHT: *This folding bed was kept in the living room and pulled down when needed. It comes from the Summer House in Lee, New Hampshire, dated c 1740. (The American Museum in Britain.)*

BELOW LEFT: *Federal mahogany secretary-bookcase made by Ebenezer Eustis of Salem, Massachusetts and dated 1808.*

FURNITURE: BEDS AND DAYBEDS

In the early 17th century, bed hangings were about the only important textiles in the colonies, one of the few items of luxury that a settler's family might have brought from the old country. So treasured were they that they feature in many an inventory and will, but, unfortunately, no examples survive. At this time, the colonial house was still a fairly basic box, in which the upstairs was used for sleeping, dining and storage. The family would be lucky to boast one 'best' bed, with several trundles brought out at night (these were mere frames with ropes or cross slats supporting a straw or feather mattress). The best beds could be either low- or high-post, made in oak, pine or maple; the fashion changed little throughout the 17th century. For privacy, curtains were sometimes suspended from the ceiling; later these were affixed to the corners of the bed. Although the more affluent would have brought their bed hangings with them, the ordinary colonists had to content themselves with those of the homespun variety.

In the 1670s, the daybed came into vogue. The first examples were in the Carolean or Charles II style, with caning on the adjustable back and the

seat. The eight turned legs were connected by ornate 'Flemish' rails and ended in small ball feet. In a short time, however, the crested rails gave way to simple turned stretchers, the legs sometimes reduced to six, the feet sometimes adopting the Spanish mode of the William and Mary style. Such pieces carried into the Queen Anne period, with the design modified to include cabriole legs and a bowed top rail. But it did not outlast the greater concentration on case pieces that came with the later Queen Anne and Chippendale periods. It would make a brief reappearance in the form of the Roman banquet couch, a fashionable New York piece at the height of the Greek and Empire vogue (*c* 1825–35). This was in truth more a sofa than a daybed, and is usually considered as such.

Although the essential character of the bed had altered little, by the first quarter of the 18th century, the establishment of the bedroom as a specfic place for sleeping allowed change to begin gradually. The bed began to dominate the room; as ceilings became higher, the bedposts increased in height. A few high-post beds were made with cabriole legs ending in pad or even claw-and-ball feet, the posts supporting a tester or straight oblong canopy with hangings of wool, crewelwork or linen. By 1750, the curtains at the foot of the bed were sometimes omitted, allowing the two posts to be exposed. Consequently they became more ornamental, taller and fluted. The 'Chippendale' makers produced beds in mahogany, cherry or maple, depending on the area, with a headboard of the same wood.

The Sheraton-style four-poster bed had two personalities. The first was elegant and stiff, with an oblong canopy and the taffeta curtains short all around, except at the head where they extended down behind the bolster. Highly carved and gilded posts supported a cornice painted and gilded with classical themes. The second variation, while often termed a 'field bed' after its military derivation, was actually the more feminine of the two. Shorter posts carried a curved canopy covered with openwork drapery of knotted cotton or mesh. Found particularly in Virginia and the Southern states, it has remained in the popular mind the archetypal American canopy bed.

The Empire furniture of the 1830s offered Americans the 'sleigh' or French bed, usually made in highly figured and polished rosewood or mahogany. The head- and footboards were curled over and carved with leaves and swags; the sides cradling the mattress were often scalloped and carved as well. In the most 'imperial' mode, the bed was literally 'crowned' by a tester, either placed over the head of the bed or horizontally.

The enthusiasm for revivals continued with the Rococo and Renaissance styles (*c* 1850–70), when the influence of John Henry Belter was felt strongly in the overpoweringly tall headboards, standing higher than a man and encrusted with flowers, fruit and leaves. Even the footboard groaned under

ABOVE: *A 'Chippendale' mahogany four-poster bedstead, c 1760–80. (Christie's, New York.)*

RIGHT: *Texas made walnut and pine bed, 1861, by Johann Umland, a German immigrant. (Winedale Museum, Roundtop, Texas.)*

FACING PAGE: *Mahogany Philadelphia bed, 1835. The hangings are reproductions of the originals. (Ladies' Hermitage Association.)*

carving. The motifs were repeated in other pieces of bedroom furniture, all of which formed a suite. The Rococo beds of Prudent Mallard (1809-79) of New Orleans were among the most ornate pieces of furniture ever made.

TOP LEFT: *Queen Anne/William and Mary transitional daybed, c 1740– 50. (The American Museum in Britain.)*

TOP RIGHT: *Queen Anne/'Chippendale' transitional daybed of red-painted maple, c 1760. (The American Museum in Britain.)*

CENTER: *Rosewood bed made by John Henry Belter, c 1860. The bed can be set up and dismantled simply and without tools. (Brooklyn Museum.)*

BELOW: *Oak and pine Bible box of the mid 17th century. It is scratched with the initials AG and the date 1644.*

FACING PAGE: *Press cupboard. made 1665–75, of oak, maple and pine. The variety of ornamentation suggests that the cupboard was produced by several artisans working in concert under the direction of one master. (Wadsworth Atheneum.)*

FURNITURE: BOXES, CHESTS AND CUPBOARDS

Bible boxes and chests number among the earliest pieces of American furniture that have come down to us. Leaving aside the crude wooden beds, stools and tables that were necessary for everyday life, the small boxes and somewhat larger chests were among the first pieces consciously chosen to be decorated for beauty and effect.

The ornate boxes, usually of pine or a soft fruit-wood, have been called book, Bible, desk or writing boxes, and a few even have slanted lids, as if to be used as a desk. Most date from between 1660 and 1700 and, outside of tables, they provided the only writing surface available until the desk-on-frame appeared toward the end of the 17th century. They were used to store reading and writing materials, as well as other small household valuables. Their designs were generally chip-cut, although the occasional example with finer background cutaway carving has also been found. The most frequent motifs found on the boxes are geometric shapes such as stars, sunbursts and lunettes, as well as floral fantasies like tulips, rosettes and hearts. The style of 'Frisian' chip carving popular along the Atlantic coast, as well as the painted carved scenes on other boxes, have all pointed to early Dutch craftsmen as their creators, but this is not a foregone conclusion.

The boxes could not hold all the necessities of a settler's life, however, and by the 1640s the clumsy six-board oak chest with a hinged lid was used to

store clothes and linens. Such chests even made the journey from England with the family, used as luggage to transport its worldly goods. But as early as 1650, Massachusetts and Connecticut craftsmen were succumbing to the urge to carve, and soon the slightly sunken oak panels were displaying elaborate intaglio designs. The pine top, however, was left plain, to allow the piece to double as a table or bench when needed.

ABOVE: *Hadley type chest with drawer, made in the Connecticut River Valley around 1680–1710. One of three known samples incorporating the Hadley carved motif within octagonal molded panels. (Bernard and S. Dean Levy, Inc, New York.)*

The typical 'blanket' or clothes chest stood about 2½ ft (75 cm) high and was between 4 and 5 ft (120 and 150 cm) long. Floral carving enlivened the front panels and sometimes those on the side, but animal and human forms never intruded. Decoration was usually two-dimensional and unsophisticated, wherein lies such a piece's charm.

The oak chests produced in the century between 1650 and 1750 usually fall into one of three groups. The 'Hartford,' 'Connecticut,' or 'Sunflower' chest is so-called because it was confined mainly to the Hartford/Wethersfield area of Connecticut, along the river of the same name; it also displays a grouping of three carved sunflowers (although some say they are rosettes) on the central panel, flanked on either side by a tulip-and-leaf scrolled panel. Two full-width drawers lie below the panels, with applied oval turtleback bosses and turned knobs. In addition, a variety of shaped split black spindles divides the panels and fronts, the stiles and the middle of the drawers. Sometimes attributed to Nicholas Disbrowe (1612/13–83), these chests were produced between 1660 and 1680.

The 'Hadley' chest is also often attributed to Disbrowe, but today it is more often credited to his grandnephew, Captain John Allis (1642–91) of Hadley, a town that lies on the Massachusetts side

ABOVE: *Blanket chest or 'mule' chest, made in New England between 1740 and 1760. (Sotheby's, New York.)*

RIGHT: *An early 18th-century painted standing corner cubboard with glazed upper door and reeded columns. The lower doors have fielded panels and the original 'H' hinges. (Colonial Williamsburg Foundation.)*

of the Connecticut River. Allis could have produced no more than a handful of the chests himself, although there are over 120 on record. Like the previous example, the Hadley chest has three panels and two drawers beneath, but the carving is in flatter relief and covers the entire front with a welter of leaves and plants in almost abstract profusion, although a characteristic tulip-and-bud pattern may often be discerned. In many cases initials are incorporated into the design – presumably when the piece was a wedding gift or 'hope' chest; very occasionally an entire name appears, as in the famous Mary Pease chest of 1714. The span of these chests was from about 1660 to 1750.

The third type, the Guildford chest, was atypical in that it was not carved. Rather, a polychrome design of foliage and flowers covered the entire chest, from the single wide front panel to the single central drawer, and two oblong side panels. This was the one chest in which wildlife featured, since a large bird silhouette was sometimes included on the side panels. The Dutch-German influence is pervasive and irrefutable. These Connecticut chests are rarer than the other two and are sometimes associated with Dutch-style dower chests.

For larger and more prosperous households there were the large oak court and press cupboards. These pieces were closely related to their Tudor and Jacobean cousins across the ocean although the colonial touch is still individualistic. Typically these cupboards were divided roughly in half horizontally, with the upper section usually set back

ABOVE: *A Federal giltwood overmantel mirror, c 1805. (Christies, New York.)*

FACING PAGE, TOP LEFT: *Mahogany mirror with scrolled border, made in Philadelphia c 1750–91. (The American Museum in Britain.)*

FACING PAGE, TOP RIGHT: *Queen Anne candle arm mirror, c 1710–30. (The American Museum in Britain.)*

FACING PAGE, BELOW LEFT: *A pine framed mirror from Pennsylvania, with a rural scene painted on the glass, c 1830. (The American Museum in Britain.)*

FACING PAGE, BELOW RIGHT: *Convex mirror, made around 1800–30. (The American Museum in Britain.)*

and framed between large turned posts at the corners. The American court cupboard has an open shelf above either a cupboard or a combination of drawers and cupboards. Sometimes the shelf incorporates a trapezoid-shaped cupboard compartment. The press cupboard has a more closed appearance, with a flat-fronted large cupboard placed above two to three wide drawers. Split spindles and bosses face the stiles of the case and sometimes divide the doors of the upper cupboard. Paneling, lavish inlay and occasional carving are the main decorative ploys used on these pieces, which were made between 1670 and 1700.

FURNITURE: MIRRORS

The earliest account of a mirror in the American colonies appears in the 1644 inventory of the estate of Joanna Cummings, at a time when all mirror glass was imported from England. Usually found in the hall, although very occasionally in the bedchamber, mirrors were very much luxuries, and those few homes that had one had *only* one. Even after 1675, it was unusual to find a family that could boast a larger number.

The advent of the William and Mary style in the colonies (*c* 1698–1700) saw the looking glass become more widespread – although its value and the fact that all silvered glass still had to make the journey across the Atlantic meant that examples were inevitably small. In wealthier homes, the simple square molded frame developed into scrolled versions with veneered crests above the glass. The richest specimens were executed in walnut, but fashionable versions were made in pine, painted to simulate tortoiseshell.

The first truly fine mirrors in America were produced during the Queen Anne period, although the glass itself continued to be imported from abroad. The fashion was for long, narrow mirrors to show off against the vertical paneling in prominent homes, but even the accomplished mirror-glass makers of Europe could not produce plate glass large enough to fulfill the ambitions of their customers at home and abroad, which extended to mirrors over 5 ft (1.5 m) in length. The looking glass was therefore usually divided into two parts, with no molding masking the join. The upper section was curved to fit the 'S'-shaped frame, which was a marriage of walnut and gesso-carved ornament, sometimes enriched with brass sconces. By 1720 the cove molding around the mirror had changed to a channeled molding, and a scrolled skirt was added to the bottom of the mirror. An alternative to the wood and gilt style was the japanned mirror, with Oriental and European designs in gold against a black or, less frequently, a cerulean blue, background.

ABOVE: *Wooden gilded mirror with eagle cresting, c 1800–10. (Hirschl and Adler Galleries, New York.)*

As the years progressed to mid-century, the looking glass became ever more common, as well as more expensive and more ornate. No longer were the majority of framed looking glasses imported. By 1750 nearly every colonial home possessed at least one mirror, and there were many types to choose from. The hall and bedchamber mirrors were joined by styles designed specifically for the overmantel – known as a chimney glass – and to accompany the newly fashionable pairs of pier tables that were placed between windows in the most elegant homes.

With the ascendancy of Philadelphia as the capital of fine furniture design, mahogany replaced walnut as the favored wood. Inner borders against the beveled glass were carved and gilded, and the central cresting above the glass often contained the vignette of a gilded shell, at first solid, later pierced. Many of these mirrors were still very large and required two pieces of glass, but the size of mirror glass was increasing and it was now possible to produce respectably sized mirrors in one piece. A number of these were in the so-called 'architectural' style, with extravagant molding and carved and gilt scrollwork. Leaves, flowers, fruit, birds, shells, phoenixes and griffins were let loose around the borders, becoming ever more exuberant as the Rococo taste took over. The pediments were crowned with cartouches, vases, papier-mâché figures and three-dimensional flowers. By the last quarter of the 18th century, the looking glass had become far more than a necessity for assessing one's toilet – it was an integral part of interior decoration.

Soon after the end of Revolutionary hostilities, the new classical designs from England began to permeate colonial fashion. Oval-shaped mirrors were all the rage, both for the wall and dressing table, either mounted on its own miniature cabinet support or attached to the chest of drawers. This latter design was a particular product of the Boston and Salem schools. Wall mirrors – both the oval versions and the rival vertical styles – were surmounted by classical urns or plaster and wire ornaments in the French taste, entirely gilded. These possessed a fragile, extremely light air that particularly complemented the early 19th-century interior.

The distinctive interior decoration of the Federal period did away with the paneling of earlier days and replaced it with wallpaper, paint in light colors and elaborate plasterwork. The ceilings were higher and the windows wider, admitting more light. The style was eminently suited to the variety of mirrors designed to reflect this brightness and illuminate what had become a more open, intellectual world. The dominance of gilding, too, only served to emphasize the importance of light. The oval mirror gave way to round convex mirrors with heavy ball borders that reflected the entire room. These were usually topped by an eagle and fitted with curling sconces – yet more light! But American as these may seem, many were imported products from England and France, merely reflecting the fascination of these nations with things Greek and Roman. Horizontal mirrors in three parts spread over the chimneypiece, while vertical mirrors continued the classical mode in a less delicate way, incorporating the same heavy ball carving used on the convex mirrors, as well as rope moldings and swags. *Verre églomisé* panels continued to be in fashion for several decades, as they were on wall clocks.

After the 1840s, the mirror declined in importance as a medium for innovative design. It continued to epitomize the taste of the moment –

ABOVE: *Pennsylvania German shrank, attributed to Peter Holl III, dated 1779. With sulphur inlay. As with most shranks, this massive piece dissambles for ease of movement. (Philadelphia Museum of Art.)*

whether it be Gothic, Louis XV or XVI, or neo-Renaissance – but it became only another piece in an increasingly overcrowded interiorscape. What it lost in terms of its contribution to design, however, it gained in size. The massive mirrors that dwarfed mantels and heavy dressing tables asserted their physical dominance – and proved perfect companions for popular fashions like crinolines, top hats and bustles, all of which demanded ample space for reflection.

FURNITURE: PENNSYLVANIA DUTCH DESIGNS

'Pennsylvania Dutch' is one of those historical misnomers that has stuck through thick and thin. The 'Dutch' were actually 'Deutsch' – Rhineland Germans and German-speaking Swiss who, driven by war and persecution, emigrated to the land colonized by William Penn. In their adoptive homeland, protected by the Quaker tolerance of all god-

full dissent, they flourished. They were thrifty and hardworking, devoting their lives to cultivating the land and developing their communities. Although the 'Deutsch' were early comers to the colony and well established by the late 17th century, it was not until the mid-18th century that they began to turn their energies to the decorative arts.

Some of their best work seems to have been mustered in the period just after the Revolution, and was initially directed toward that most important part of their lives: family. In their young girlhood the daughters of these German farmers began planning for their marriage. Dower chests – usually made from pine or poplar and painted to order – were given as gifts by parents and family, so that homespun linens, quilts, coverlets, hangings and towels could be stored for future use. The type of chest was patterned on oak examples of the same period or earlier in their German homeland, but, unlike the originals, they featured little carving. Instead, motifs were painted – a gayer and less time-consuming form of decoration.

The usual background color was a soft, medium blue, although green, brown and black were used, albeit less frequently. The style of decorative overpainting was standardized and markedly naïve, echoing many of the same devices that appeared on *fractur* (baptismal certificates and other hand-lettered hand-decorated manuscripts), tin or ceramics. Symbolism played a large part in the choice: hearts signified happiness; the tree of life, mortality; stars, luck; flowers, fertility; doves, peace.

LEFT: *Pennsylvania German chest c 1780, of painted yellow pine and poplar. (Metropolitan Museum of Art, New York.)*

ABOVE: *Painted and decorated two-drawer chest c 1789 signed Johannes Rank 1789/Dauphen Co. Penn. (Christie's, New York.)*

Medieval symbols appeared as well, among them unicorns (virginity), mermaids (sexual seduction), the pelican and fish (early Christian motifs). Since the craftsmen and their families were strict ascetic Protestants, it is fair to assume that these latter decorations were retained as part of their unconscious heritage, their deeper meanings largely unappreciated. Many of the chests carry the owner's name and or initials and the date.

In addition to the dower chests, a few other pieces of furniture were typical articles in a Pennsylvania Dutch household. In addition to tables, plank-bottomed chairs and beds – all usually painted and some charmingly decorated – other objects included hanging wall cabinets and corner cupboards, the latter often painted red; unpainted doughboys (large chests on legs for mixing and kneading bread); heavy wardrobes called *schranks,* which were painted and streaked, and pie 'safes' or kitchen cupboards with decorative pierced-tin panels. Despite their amateur creation and rough finish, these pieces betray a distinctive American character that has guaranteed them a prominent place in our national affections.

FURNITURE: THE SHAKER TRADITION

Shaker furniture has been called 'religion in wood,' and the amount of critical adulation it has received in the last hundred years certainly bears out its capacity for conversion. Governed by the strict but humanitarian tenets of their faith, the Shakers created pieces transcending the bounds of the movement – and becoming arguably the most internationally recognized and admired style of American furniture.

RIGHT: *This three-step Shaker stool, for a high bed or a library, was made in New Lebanon in New York State and dates to 1830. (The American Museum in Britain.)*

ABOVE: *A daybed in the Gathering Room at Hancock, Massachusetts. (Michael Freeman.)*

LEFT: *A long-case clock made by Benjamin Youngs at Watervliet. (Paul Rocheleau.)*

The church owed its founding to one woman, Ann Lee, a young worker in the textile mills of Manchester, England. In 1758 she joined a Quaker Society that had been much influenced by an evangelical French sect, and which was in turn impressed when Ann herself began receiving revelations concerning the Second Coming, celibacy and mode of worship. The latter was highly emotional and frenetic, involving dancing and shaking, which gave the breakaway sect under her direction – The United Society of Believers in Christ's Second Coming – their vernacular nickname, 'The Shakers.' Labeled as heretics, the group fled to America in 1774, where Ann died 10 years later. But her little society had flourished and made converts, and by 1780 had founded their first colony, in Niskayuna, near Albany in Upstate New York. Soon the first fully organized community – and along with the one in Hancock, Massachusetts, probably the most famous – was established at Lebanon, New York, in 1788. Eventually there were 18 Shaker communities, spread from as far north as Maine to as far west as Ohio and as far south as Kentucky. At the height of their popularity in the mid-19th century the Shakers claimed some 6,000 members, but the celibate life and 20th-century mores meant a consistently dwindling membership. Today their villages are bereft of followers, although preserved as historical monuments.

In their colonies, the members made all their own furniture. They believed the designs for their rockers, chairs, chests, tables, desks, beds, cupboards and washstands came from the Lord himself and were transmitted by angels to the hands of their craftsmen. Every piece embodied the precepts that the Shakers held so tenaciously. Chief among them were the principles of 1) order and use, 2) separation from the world, 3) separation of the sexes, 4) community of goods, and 5) perfectionism.

Order was inherent, since each piece was designed as an inanimate servant to order. Drawers

LEFT: *This chest of drawers has an unusual top with a folding leaf. (American Museum in Britain.)*

BELOW: *Shaker rocking chair, c 1840. (The American Museum in Britain.)*

and cupboards provided storage space to the best possible effect; drop leaves accommodated both the need for extra working space and the lack of standing space; peg boards on the wall removed extraneous chairs from the floor when not in use; and nest boxes with fingered join construction allowed the smaller necessities of daily life to be filed away until needed.

Use and separation from the world went together in Shaker design. 'Functionalism' was their creed long before the word was applied to modern furniture. Fussy decoration and cluttered lines were taboo and, indeed, no concessions were made to fashions of the time. Rather, the appearance of a piece was governed by its use. Once a satisfactory shape was achieved that was strong, easy to make and served its purpose well, it became the accepted design for that piece, a design that was then shared with all the other Shaker communities. Of course some regional variations did manifest themselves – the makers, after all, were artisans, not automatons – but the basic shape of the particular types of Shaker furniture varied astonishingly little.

Separation of the sexes and community of goods were also intertwined, since all furniture was dedicated to communal use and made by a *community* of craftsmen. Private ownership and the worldy sin of selfishness were anathema to the Shakers, but at the same time the separate needs of the sexes were appreciated and provided for. Chairs for sisters were lighter and smaller than those for brothers; women's tables were often lower and their chests of drawers had more compartments. Sewing stands

RIGHT: *New Mexico Spanish colonial grain chest and detail of the latch. (From the collection of Shirley and Ward Alan Minge; Robert Reck Photography.)*

FACING PAGE, FAR LEFT: *Shaker boxes such as these were used for all general purposes, and were sold singly or in matched sets. (Thomas K. Woodard Antiques, New York.)*

FACING PAGE, TOP RIGHT: *A cupboard and case of drawers from New Lebanon, New York, c 1825–50. (Paul Rocheleau.)*

FACING PAGE, BELOW RIGHT: *A washstand with a hinged pail stand that can be swung out to allow easier access to the pail of dirty water. (Paul Rocheleau.)*

were built whose drawers slid out from the sides, thus enabling sisters to work facing one another.

Finally, perfectionism – or purity of life – was the result of this avid attention to the other four principles. 'Anything may, with strict propriety, be called perfect, which perfectly answers the purpose for which it was designed,' wrote Seth Wells, in *The Laws of the Millennium,* one of the Shaker 'bibles'. That they succeeded in this aim was acknowledged by early visitors to their colonies, like the writer Harriet Martineau; by later arbiters of taste, like the innovative architect Louis Sullivan, and today by the curators of the world's greatest museums, in which exhibitions of Shaker design command definitive catalogs and attract enormous crowds.

FURNITURE: THE SOUTHWESTERN STYLE

The only two types of indigenous furniture designs in America with inescapably ethnic roots (taking the tradition of English-French inspiration as the norm) were the gaily carved and painted chests, cupboards and dressers of the Pennsylvania Germans (or 'Dutch') and the somber, spartan Spanish-influenced cabinetwork of the Southwest – New Mexico, Arizona, Texas and, to a lesser extent, California.

The main period of creative activity was 1800 to 1880, a time when the area was effectively isolated from the fashions and comforts of the Eastern settlements. When Mexico declared its independence from Spain in 1822, the repercussions were few. The well-to-do residents of California continued to obtain many of their household furnishings from Mexico, where skilled workmanship modeled itself on the fashions of the Old World. The haciendas were furnished comfortably, as were the missions.

While the Spanish missions were not rich, the best of the local craftsmen were pleased to do their most creative work for the glory of God. Thus it is to the missions we owe the wonderful painted wooden candlestands, ornamented with ball carvings and large-petaled flowers; confessionals whose

curved pediments dazzle with sunbursts of dot and tear carving, ornate wooden grilles and crosses; and prayer kneelers, monstrances and tabernacles – all alive with coarse but vital carving. There were even special chairs for the priest or visiting bishop to sit on during the celebration of the Mass.

But such lavish decoration did not hold for the majority of the furniture in the Spanish-speaking areas. The poverty of existence in the New Mexican region (which for our purposes also includes Arizona, Texas and lower Colorado) was pervasive and largely unaltered over the years; this was reflected by the primitiveness of the furnishings. There were few tools from which to choose: the small Spanish axe, the chisel, knife, awl, adze and handsaw. No sawmill opened in the area until the 1870s; planks were hand-hewn and smoothed by sandstone rubbing. The main woods were the readily available yellow pine, and, to a much lesser extent, juniper, mesquite and cottonwood. In 18th- and early 19th-century chests, nails were not used, but rather mortise-and-tenon joints, dovetailing and dowels were the norm. Handwrought nails were used for repairs and for later pieces.

New Mexican chairs, benches and settees are among the most common furniture pieces extant today. The usual chair form had either a plank or rawhide seat, the latter secured with large brass studs. Construction was rigid and unyielding; the legs were square, unadorned posts and the backs were horizontal wooden slats or tooled leather. A seat of honor, reserved for important guests or the visiting padre, might evince some abstract curling carving on the back, apron and/or stretcher, but more common was the rugged sawtooth back and stretcher, a design that also appeared on table stretchers and chest aprons.

ABOVE: *Carved chest from New Mexico, made in the mid/late 18th century of carved pine. (The American Museum in Britain.)*

LEFT: *New Mexico Spanish colonial chair. (From the collection of Shirley and Ward Alan Minge; Robert Reck Photography.)*

Large pine chests were used for storage and were usually quite simple, with molded panels and plain square legs. Smaller chests were sometimes more like boxes, mounted on their own stands. A rarer form was the painted dower chest, based on an earlier form from Chihuahua, Mexico, which 19th-century artisans had seen in the homes of some older families. But whereas the original chests were the work of trained craftsmen like those who supplied the haciendas in California, the native efforts of the New Mexican amateurs were crudely painted and finished. But their appeal is none the less for that, and they are among the most sought-after of Southwestern antiques.

Another form of storage was offered by the *trasero*, a large pine two-story cupboard on legs, with hand-carved spindles forming a grille on the upper doors. The classic form has access to drawers on the front and back of the piece, with the

TOP LEFT: *New Mexico Spanish colonial table. (From the collection of Shirley Ward and Ward Alan Minge; Robert Reck Photography.)*

CENTER LEFT: *Painted chest on legs, New Mexico 1828–45. (The American Museum in Britain.)*

RIGHT: *A Trastero cupboard with spindled upper doors, from the mid 19th century. (The American Museum in Britain.)*

ABOVE: *A chair with chip carving, New Mexico, early 19th century. (The American Museum in Britain.)*

LEFT: *A missal stand, typically made of pine. Made in Morada in New Mexico c 1900. (The American Museum in Britain.)*

RIGHT: *A New Mexico Spanish colonial cupboard. (From the collection of Shirley Ward Alan Minge; Robert Reck Photography.)*

'drawer' on the opposite side actually a blind. This was often the most imposing piece in the house, covered with gesso and painted with figures in bright colors. Less gaudy decoration is found on some of the oldest pieces and on examples from the poorest households.

After 1840, the intrusion of Eastern fashions resulted in less 'pure' pieces. This was reflected in 'Empire'-influenced chairs, the appearance of chests of drawers and taller tables, and other small bastardizations of the Spanish-Mexican style. But lovers of the Southwestern tradition find these aberrations of interest in and of themselves, as long as the pieces continue to exhibit the unself-conscious naïveté of the traditional forms.

FURNITURE: ARTS AND CRAFTS, 1880–1920

American furniture design of the late 19th and early 20th centuries experienced a sea change, breaking the pattern of traditional development in which styles ebbed and flowed, one into another, to produce a kind of decorative evolution. By the 1880s, the eclecticism of the Victorian age had so fragmented the concept of what furniture should be or achieve – or even look like – that 'schools' sprang up in different corners of the United States, all trying to find, in their own way, the true path to interior enlightenment in its most literal sense.

In place of historicism was an interest in straight lines and unfussy surfaces. Wood was seen as an organic element akin to stone and treated to the same shallow relief carving and blunt edges. In academic terms, the designers of the Chicago School and the Prairie School set the pace. The

TOP: *A teak settle by Charles and Henry Green, 1906, deriving its form from the functional pieces of the early settlers.*

ABOVE: *This c 1910 oak hall bench is typical of the work of Gustave Stickley, using local wood in an austere style.*

RIGHT: *Frank Lloyd Wright writing table and chair, made from American walnut and enamelled steel, c 1936.*

intimations of reform reverberated loudly there, disturbed by the breath of fresh air in architecture, which blew across all the decorative arts. In Chicago itself were the practices of Jenny, Burnham & Root, Henry Hobson Richardson (1838–86) and, most famous of all, Adler and Sullivan. In 1889 Louis H. Sullivan (1856–1924) took on the young and ambitious Frank Lloyd Wright (1869–1959) as a junior member of his firm; four years later, in 1893, Wright had opened his own business. His so-called 'Oak Park Period' – named after the site of his own Illinois house, for which he designed the furniture – extended from that date until 1910. At the Oak Park residence, and in all the other houses he designed, the furnishings were seen as a natural outgrowth of the building itself. He despised artifice and 'tampering with nature.' His advice – 'Bring out the nature of materials, let their nature intimately into your scheme. Strip the wood of varnish and let it alone – stain it . . . Go to the woods and fields for color schemes . . .' echoed through Chicago and westward across the prairies, where other architect-designers were attempting their own interpretation of reform.

ABOVE: *Oak spindle chairs and table made by Frank Lloyd Wright c 1901.*

Some of the Prairie School members had been students at the foot of Sullivan at about the same time as Wright. But whereas Wright went so far toward the terse and clean-cut that he finally decreed that machines did the job better than man, architect-designers George Grant Elmslie and George Washington Maher did not scorn decorative detail if it was integral to the piece. Working first for the architectural practice of Bauer and Hill, and then for Chicago's largest firm, J. L. Silsbee, Maher chose strong lines and massive proportions for his pieces. But he also showed that finding a new aesthetic did not demand a complete break with the past. Obvious respect for the medieval and Renaissance traditions – apparent in the scrolling stiles and animal heads that adorn some of his best works – is spiced with delight in Oriental forms. In addition, his influence on other designers of the Midwest was highly important.

Meanwhile, while architect-designers turned academic ideals into reality for the few, there were more commercial outlets riding along on the new wave. The creations of these firms were still expensive, since they clung to the tenets of Arts

LEFT: *Honduras mahogany and teak chest with carved ebony panel by C. & H. Greene, California 1907–09.*

ABOVE: *An oak fall-front desk by Stickly, c 1904. The panelled fall is inlaid with stylized motifs in pewter and various light woods.*

LEFT: *An art nouveau armchair by Greene & Greene. c 1908.*

RIGHT: *Purcell and Elmslie armchair; oak with the original upholstery and brass tacks; date unknown. (Hirschl & Adler Galleries, New York.)*

and Crafts excellence, but they were sales companies, not architectural firms, and there was a growing core of well-off businessmen to buy their products. Chief among these companies was Herter Brothers in New York, as well as Isaac E. Scott and the Tobey Furniture Company, both in Chicago. Furnishing the Jackson Boulevard home of the Chicago industrialist Henry Lee Borden had a large part in making the latter firm's name.

While all this was happening west of the Appalachians, other movements were afoot in New York State. In 1898 Gustav Stickley (1857–1942) began designing his craftsman furniture in Eastwood, a Syracuse suburb, stating his aim that 'furniture should be durable, comfortable and fitted for the place it has to occupy and the work it has to do'. His furniture was made of native American hardwoods, the stuffed pieces covered in leather, canvas or plain cloth. The fittings were of copper or iron. His designs were long-lasting – his reclining chair, patented in 1901, was still being manufactured unchanged in 1913 – and much imitated. Although he took the precaution of having three trademarks on every piece of his furniture, in 1915 he was bankrupt by those same cheaply and widely-produced imitations.

The simple oak tables, benches, chairs and bookcases of Elbert Hubbard (1856–1915) and his community of craftsmen in Aurora, New York, were even less conspicuous. His group was christened the Roycrofters and its members saw themselves as the latter-day inheritors of the William Morris tradition. Together the works of Hubbard and Stickley are referred to as 'Mission furniture' – so-called at first because 'they had a mission to perform'. However, the name gradually took on the connotations of the California missions, with whose simplicity the brown-stained wood seemed much in sympathy.

In fact the appellation should have been given to the designs of Charles Sumner Greene (1868–1957) and Henry Mather Greene (1870–1954), two Californian brothers and architectural graduates whose pieces also echoed the calm and Old West values of the Franciscan missions. Rather unfortunately, their work is sometimes known today as 'the California bungalow style'. Like the architects in the Midwest, they designed houses and the furniture to go in them. Their grand Spanish-style mansions in Pasadena and San Marino were made complete by the inclusion of their lovely walnut furniture. Unlike the others, they used inlay – in fruitwood and semiprecious stones – and ebony pegs to cover their joinery. But they embraced other artisans in their vision: Stickley furniture, Rockwood pottery and Tiffany glass were among the items that adorned Greene houses.

C H A P T E R T W O

CLOCKS

Suiting the time to the place: creating an affordable and distinctively American style of timepiece.

ABOVE: *Federal stained maple shelf clock, Maine c 1815–25. (Christie's, New York.)*

LONG-CASE (GRANDFATHER) CLOCKS

LEFT: *Long-case Tiffany clock with Near East and Indian motifs; mahogany and brass, c 1880. (Metropolitan Museum of Art, New York.)*

Clocks and timepieces were among those luxuries – along with guns and glass for windows and domestic use – that the earliest New World settlers brought with them on the ships from England. Those who could not afford them hardly considered them necessities; only the wealthiest thought them worth the effort to drag halfway across the world. Even after living for a generation in North America, in the 1680s and 1690s colonists were still largely importing clocks from England. With only two or three exceptions no clocks made before 1700 in America are known to exist today.

By 1715 there were several clockmakers at work, first mainly concentrated in Philadelphia, but then spreading out to Newport, Boston and other centers. The majority of these 18th-century clocks were of the long-case (or grandfather or 'tall-case') variety. The most admired of American clock craftsmen, David Rittenhouse (1732–96), worked in Norristown, near Philadelphia, between 1750 and 1790, producing several outstanding examples that are today the pride of American museums. The skilled clockmaker Thomas Harland (d 1807) emigrated from England to Norwich, Connecticut, in 1773, and his apprentice, Daniel Burnap (1760–1838), became among the most highly regarded of the Connecticut school long-case clockmakers (he moved from East Windsor, Connecticut, to Andover, Massachusetts, *c* 1800). Clocks by such excellent makers were made to order by hand and fitted to a mahogany case that had also been made in the shop. Most had brass eight-day movements, though there are the exceptional 34-hour versions. The dials were of brass with brass spandrels and other ornamental details.

In contrast, some innovative makers were beginning to look for less costly alternatives, making functional pieces with cog wheels of cherry mounted on an oak plate, contained in an attractive but simple case. The Cheney Brothers of East Hartford, Connecticut, are hailed as making the earliest of these existing Connecticut wooden movements, in about 1745. Although cheaply and sometimes crudely made, they are almost as keenly sought after as their more sophisticated brethren. Other early makers include Gideon Rich and John Roberts.

Among the apprentices of Benjamin Cheney was Benjamin Willard (1740–1803), who, with his three brothers, went on to revolutionize the clock industry of eastern Massachusetts, southern New Hampshire and Rhode Island. Although influenced by the Cheneys, the brothers and their factories never made any wooden clocks, concentrating instead on finely made brass movements. From

BELOW: *Federal long-case painted clock, made in Connecticut c 1825. It was painted by R. Cole who stencilled 'R Cole Painter' on the base in gold. (Sotheby's, New York.)*

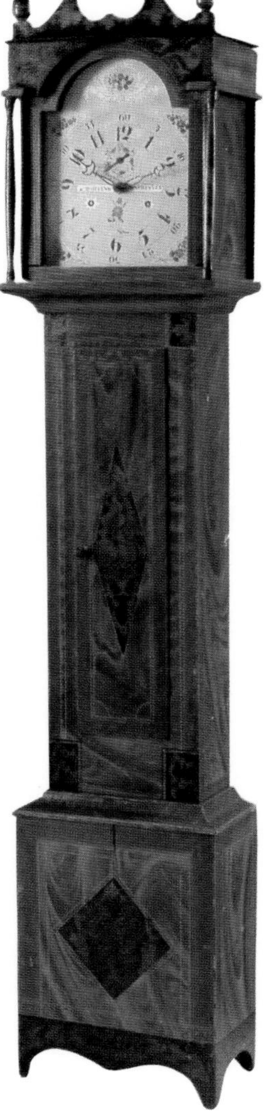

ABOVE: *Joseph Ives mirror clock in gilt gesso frame, made c 1820 in Bristol, CT. (American Clock and Watch Museum.)*

LEFT: *Rittenhouse clock. (Drexel University.)*

1765 on they produced many types and styles of timepiece, most notable among them their long-case and banjo clocks.

Mass-production in the modern style began with the Connecticut clockmaker Eli Terry (1772–1852), who set up his shop and factory in 1793 (after an apprenticeship with Daniel Burnap), installed steam power to fuel his works in 1803 and accepted an order for 4,000 wooden long-case clock movements in 1806. He established the first assembly line for clock production in America to fill the order and make his fortune. The majority of his movements were sold without cases, which could then be made to the specifications of the customer; an even cheaper solution was to simply hang up the movement uncased – this was known as a 'wag-on-the-wall'.

By the second decade of the 19th century, several makers had taken up Terry's ideas and were making wooden clocks, long-case and otherwise. But with the decline of Chippendale style furnishings, the long-case gave pride of place to several new rivals.

ABOVE: *Seth Thomas Clock Co., Thomaston, CT; gilt column model one-day weight-driven shelf clock, c 1870. (American Clock and Watch Museum.)*

LEFT: *Banjo clock, made c 1830. (Taylor B. Williams Antiques, Chicago, Illinois.)*

CLOCKS: WALL CLOCKS

Although Dutch and English brass wag-on-the-wall clocks had been imported into the American colonies since the mid-17th century, it was not until the middle of the next century that homegrown artisans assayed making the same products in America. Eli Terry's mass-produced wooden works (*c*1806 and after) were often hung without cases, and by 1815 several makers were copying his methods to supply cheap, utilitarian wag-on-the-wall pieces to a growing clientele.

Meanwhile, Simon Willard (1753–*c*1845), perhaps the most renowned of the four Willard Brothers, had been developing a more sophisticated wall-mounted 'Improved Timepiece.' Although early examples exist before 1800, he did not patent his invention until 1802. The movements were brass, the eight-day weight-driven pendulum between 20 and 26 in (50 and 66 cm) long. The wooden case consisted of a long upper section surmounted by the clock face and containing the pendulum suspension and escapement, while the square lower section was fronted by a glass-painted panel, or 'tablet,' and contained the pendulum weight. It was only in the latter part of the 19th century that it acquired the appellation 'banjo clock'. So popular did the shape become that 'banjos' were made by hundreds of craftsmen from the early 1800s throughout the 19th century, although the most finely executed tend to be pre-1830. The design lent itself to many variations. More deliberate faking has probably occurred with this type of clock than with any other American variety.

Two more exuberant styles, closely allied to the banjo in shape, movement and period, were the 'girandole' and the lyre, both of which flourished between 1815 and 1840. The design of the latter is credited to Aaron Willard Jr., nephew of Simon, and was taken up by many Massachusetts craftsmen. The girandole was the invention of Lemuel Curtis (1790–1851) of Massachusetts. Taking its name from the extravagant girandole mirrors of the period, it is considered among the most beautiful of American clocks. Fine examples are extremely difficult to find today and command high prices.

Plainer clocks, rectangular with the familiar lower glass panel, were made in mahogany and in rosewood by several other firms, principally in Connecticut, from the mid-19th century onward. They could either be used as shelf or wall clocks, and ogee molding distinguished many of the better examples. Generally speaking, after 1840–50, wall clocks were exceeded in popularity by the shelf variety, and those wall clocks that were produced usually followed the fashion dictates of the more widespread type.

ABOVE: *Tiffany mantel set; ormolu and marble with Egyptian motifs. Made in New York c 1885. (Metropolitan Museum of Art, New York.)*

CLOCKS: SHELF CLOCKS

After the long-case or grandfather clock, the American shelf clock – in all its manifestations – is the most fertile field for the horological student. Its earliest versions were a concession to space and expense, since the larger clocks were difficult to import from England and skilled craftsmen were few in the colonies. It was not until the second decade of the 18th century that a few names came to the fore. But since the long-case clock demanded a rich clientele, craftsmen began to experiment with other styles that made use of their skills but were more affordable and consistent with the distinctive American interiors.

One solution was the so-called Massachusetts shelf clock, produced by members of the Willard family as an alternative to their pricier long-cases. Made from around 1800 to 1830, they are sometimes called 'case-on-case' or 'box-on-box,' a fair description of the basic construction of these brass movement pieces.

In contrast, the pillar-and-scroll clock of Eli Terry and his sons (*c*1817 and after) combined the wooden movements he had pioneerred in his long-case pieces with a small walnut or mahogany case, between 20 and 40 in (50 and 100 cm). Turned or carved posts flanked the sides, while a broken arch or double scroll characterized the top. The door contained a glass window above the glass-painted tablet. By the 1820s, other makers in Connecticut, Massachusetts and Pennsylvania were following Terry's lead and the trend continued until the 1840s, to be overtaken by other styles echoing current fashions in furniture – the stenciled shelf clock in the style of Hitchcock (*c*1825–40), the carved or marquetry beehive (*c*1850–60), the Gothic steeple (*c*1850–60), and the 'O.G.' clock, so-named because of its ogee-molded front. These last were in vogue from about 1840 into the 20th century, growing more massive in size and decoration as the decades progressed. The changes in style were accompanied by a change in movement construction; after 1840 wooden cogs and movements gave way to rolled brass and, soon after, to steel springs, which opened the way for true mass-production.

In addition to wooden cases, other materials were called into use as they came into fashion in other furnishings. Papier-mâché enjoyed popularity *c*1860–70, usually in the form of small boudoir clocks, while iron, brass and porcelain were all used for mantel clocks in the later 19th century. Porcelain, in particular, was favored for both boudoir and parlor clocks, the latter sometimes forming part of a garniture with companion vases.

Among the great names for the collector, congregated mainly in the first half of the 19th century, are the Willards and Terrys, together with the Jerome Brothers – Chauncey and Noble – and J. C. Brown and the Bristol Clock Company of Bristol, Connecticut.

RIGHT: *One day wood-movement clock by E. Terry & Son, Plymouth, CT, c 1830. The case decoration is influenced by stenciled furniture styles. (American Clock and Watch Museum.)*

CHAPTER THREE

SILVER

'The time is not far off when we shall have no need of foreign designers of our plate and jewelry.' Harper's Monthly *1853*

Above: *A silver porringer. (Christie's, New York.)*

ABOVE: *A two-handled cup with cover made by Jurian Blanck Jr. 1666–1699 in New York. (The Henry Francis du Pont Winterthur Museum.)*

PORRINGERS, BEAKERS AND CAUDLE CUPS

Unlike many other trades, that of the silversmith (or goldsmith, as they were then known) became established early in America. This occurred for two reasons: the eagerness of the wealthier English emigrés to establish their social status in their new country, and the importance of silver as an easily convertible asset. Like the display of jewelry on a Berber wife, silver on a colonial sideboard established the owner as a man of substance with his collateral up-front. Silver could also be rendered into coinage when needed, controls on minting being enviably lax.

The first settlers brought with them what valuables they could, and since silver was relatively light and not easily damaged, it featured largely among the items of luxury that traveled across the ocean. Goldsmiths themselves saw the 'golden' opportunity in the new country and arrived in notable numbers to establish a clientele. John Mansfield of Charlestown, Massachusetts, is known to have been plying his trade in 1634, and in the 30 years after 1650, 24 makers were registered as working in Boston alone.

Among the earliest craftsmen trained in the colonies were John Jull (1624–83) and Robert Sanderson (1608–93). Hull was trained by his half-brother Richard Storer, who had not completed his articles in London but set up shop in Boston. It was probably just after completing his apprenticeship that Hull made the tapered cylindrical beaker (the only surviving piece to bear his mark alone) that lays claim to being the only authenticated piece of pre-1650 American silver. After gaining his articles, Hull became very active both artistically and socially; by 1652 he was appointed Master of the Massachusetts Mint. This prestigious position enabled him to set up a flourishing business with his friend Robert Sanderson. Most of the silver produced by Hull and Sanderson bears the mark of both partners; the less than 40 pieces extant today survived because they were given to churches. Hull and Sanderson were also responsible for training many of the next generation of goldsmiths,

ABOVE: *Porringer made by Peter Van Inbrugh c 1710–25. It is engraved with 'P VB' in a rectangle on the base. (Mabel Brady Garvan Collection, Yale University Art Gallery.)*

RIGHT: *Tankard made by Jacob Boelen in New York, c 1685. (Brooklyn Museum.)*

including Jeremiah Dummer (1645–1718), America's first native-born craftsman; Timothy Dwight (1654–?), of whose elegant pieces only two known survive, and John Coney (1655–1722), the greatest of America's early silversmiths. After Hull's death in 1682, Sanderson worked on alone; few pieces signed singly by him exist.

While the new generation of goldsmiths was learning its craft in Boston, New York was beginning to make its own, quite different mark. In Boston, the dominant influence was English, and the silverwork echoed, albeit rather belatedly, the fashions of the most influential London makers. New York, however, was known as New Amsterdam until 1664, and the silver produced there showed Dutch inspiration, tempered by the French lines of several immigrant Huguenot craftsmen who settled in the colony. The names of these early artisans betray their origins: Jesse Kip, Koenraet Ten Eyck, Cornelius Kierstede and Cornelius Van der Burgh (1653–99), New York's first native goldsmith; their cross-influence is represented by Huguenot Bartholomew LeRoux and his Dutch-named apprentice Peter Van Dyck.

Among the articles made by these smiths and their followers were beakers, caudle cups and porringers. Some of these pieces were made expressly for churches – non-conformist in Boston and Dutch Reformed in New York – while others served a period of domestic use and were then given as generous alms or bequeathed as legacies. Beakers, tankards and caudle cups were by their nature ecclesiastical as well as domestic; in the American Protestant churches they usually replaced standing cups or chalices in services. However, porringers do not have an established church use; it is probable that their shape and popularity suggested their donation to the church plate. These shallow silver bowls with flat handles are known as porringers only in the United States; in Great Britain they are more commonly known as cupping bowls or bleeding bowls. They are particularly helpful to the student of American silver, since many are engraved with the donor's name and/or date, facilitating research into a period in which hallmarks are rare and untrustworthy.

A comparison of the styles of New York and Boston shows immediate and startling differences, intimations of which remain throughout the following 18th century. While the English-style beakers of John Coney and his Boston compatriots are restrained and elegant, those of the New Yorkers (as typified by the wonderfully engraved and embossed example by Cornelius Van der Burgh of 1685 in the Yale University Art Gallery) are extravagant and very Continental. As for the porringers, those in the Boston style usually have solid handles with embossed or incised engraving; those following the New York influence favor handles with pierced work – extravagant in the early years, mellowing to simple openwork in the 18th century.

After the straight-sided, flaring-rimmed beakers produced in the early period, Queen Anne styling introduced the curving bell shape stabilized on a molded foot. By the Federal period, the last lingering designs for these outmoded vessels had conformed to the classical ovoid shape.

SILVER: TANKARDS, CANNS AND MUGS

The greatest number of surviving early American pieces are tankards. Those produced in Boston between 1690 and 1720 have clean, pure lines, relying for their effect upon a balanced design rather than ornament. Before 1715 the cylindrical body tapered from the plain base to the flat-lidded top; after that date, the lid became dome-shaped, topped with a finial, and the body line was interrupted by a mid-band. The handle was a simple single scroll terminating in a dolphin or acanthus thumb-piece.

The most respected silversmith of this school was John Coney, whose productive life spanned three distinct styles: the Carolingian, from which survive cherub caudle cups, ornate sugar boxes and porringers; his middle William and Mary period, during which he produced monumental tankards, two-handled covered cups and the celebrated Harvard Monteith of *c*1705, and the Queen Anne style, in which he sacrificed chased decoration for the wonderfully functional pear-shaped lines that characterized the period.

By contrast, the New York tankards and pieces of the 1690 to 1720 period were larger and heavier,

ABOVE: *Pair of canns made in Boston, Massachusetts, 1750. Engraved with contemporary initials 'BSC' and below, the name 'Collins'. (The American Museum in Britain.)*

BELOW: *Cann by T. Revere (Paul Revere Jr's brother) made in Boston 1879. (The American Museum in Britain.)*

ABOVE: *Snuff box by Joseph Richardson. (Mabel Brady Garvan Collection, Yale University Art Gallery.)*

with reeded, foliate bases. When Boston deserted the flat top for a domed lid, New York remained faithful, merely adding more decoration to it. Sometimes the lid incorporated a coin inset into it, while the scroll handle might be enlivened with embossing and terminate in a corkscrew thumb-piece. An exceptionally fine example of the New York tankard by Jacobus van der Spiegel is in the Yale University Art Gallery. Other makers from the New York school of this period include the newly qualified Peter Van Dyck and Jacob Boelen.

In the last years of the 17th century, Philadelphia began producing its first pieces, including tankards and porringers. But while the tankards followed more closely the style set by New York, the old-fashioned porringers and newly fashionable teapots made there tended to take their style lead from Boston. One of the outstanding pieces of Philadelphia silver is the tankard at the Yale Art Gallery, made *c*1730 by Irish-born Philip Syng, Jr. (1703–89); other great Philadelphia makers of the 1720–70 period include Francis and Joseph Richardson, Joseph Ledel and William Vilant.

Meanwhile, Rhode Island and Connecticut, too, had begun their infant industries, combining attitudes and fashions from both the main silver centers. In the 1690s, Cesar Ghiselin, of Huguenot extraction, moved from Philadelphia to Annapolis to become Maryland's first goldsmith, while Johannis Nys moved from the same city to Delaware at the turn of the 18th century to begin the craft there. None of the provincial makers, however, was of sufficient quality to challenge the dominance of Boston, New York and eventually Philadelphia until after the War of Independence.

The Rococo style initiated in 1750 saw its characteristic pear shape adapted to the Boston tankard fairly early on, but New York clung to its Stuart style for several more years. The typically American 'cann,' or lidless mug, was also a development of this time, but by 1780 and the last sighs of the Rococo, the tankard, too, had outlived its fashion.

SILVER: CENTERPIECES, BOWLS, TUREENS AND PITCHERS

The Rococo style suited the merchant classes that were becoming influential in the flourishing colonies. It was their commercial success that aggravated dissatisfaction with British rule and taxation; there emerged a general feeling that perhaps the mother country was more of a hindrance than a help. In the period immediately before and succeeding the Revolution, the popularity of Rococo design echoed the burgeoning confidence of the Americans; the lavish shell motifs and pierced scrolls of the style

found their way into silverwork, particularly centerpieces, monteiths and other larger objects that could happily assimilate its opulence. New York makers such as Myer Myers (1723–95) and Daniel Christian Fueter (*fl*1754–76) often worked in this style, as did Philadelphia smiths Philip Hulbeart (*fl*1750–64), Joseph Richardson (1711–84), and Richard Humphreys (*fl*1771–96). The latter made the lavish urn presented to Charles Thomson, Secretary of the Continental Congress, by its members.

The Federal period is a highly important one in American history, spanning as it does the infant years of the American republic. It is also synonymous with one of the great names in American silver – Paul Revere, Jr. (1735–1818) – goldsmith and patriot. Son of Huguenot goldsmith Apollos Rivoire, who himself studied under the famous John Coney and duly anglicized his name, Paul Revere was one of the most active silversmiths in Boston, doing much subcontracted work for other masters such as Nathaniel Hurd (1729–77), son of the equally respected Jacob and brother of Benjamin; Samuel Minott (1732–1803) and John Coburn (1725–1803), as well as producing elegant pieces stamped with his own mark. As a sideline to his smithing, Revere became a dentist; as a patriot, he put his skill as an engraver to use in publishing revolutionary tracts and political cartoons. After the war he printed

ABOVE: *Two Empire sauceboats by Anthony Rasch; made in Philadelphia 1808–19. (Metropolitan Museum of Art, New York.)*

CENTER: *Tureen by William Thomson, 1809–45. (Metropolitan Museum of Art, New York.)*

BELOW: *Sauceboat by Joseph Lownes, Philadelphia c 1785. (Christie's, New York.)*

Above: *A 'monteith', or bowl used for cooling wine glasses, by John Conery. (Mabel Brady Garvan Collection, Yale University Art Gallery.)*

currency for the Continental Congress. He was a man of many talents, but his silverwork alone would have made him a great name in the annals of early American design.

Although Revere made pieces spanning all the usual items found in contemporary catalogs and daybooks – teapots, tankards, bowls, sauceboats, pitchers, etc. – his most famous piece is without a doubt the Sons of Liberty Bowl, now in the Museum of Fine Arts, Boston. Weighing 45 oz (12.7 kg), and engraved and embossed with dedications and symbols of liberty, it was commissioned by the Insurance Office of Nathaniel Barber, one of Boston's foremost citizens. Although Revere himself does not mention it at all in his daybook, it bears his unmistakeable touchmark.

The Federal style is neo-classical in feeling and, if executed with ability, it assumes a refined, elegant attitude, exercising its decorative urges in fluting, reeding and gadrooning. It was a direct contrast to the exuberant Rococo style, yet both lent themselves well to monumental pieces. Other makers who excelled in its practice include Benjamin Burt (1729–1815) and Daniel Henchman (1730–75) of Boston; Joseph Richardson, Jr. (1752–1831), and John and James Black of Philadelphia; Ephraim Brasher (1744–1810), and Daniel Van Voorhis and Gerrit Schank (partners 1791–92) of New York.

The apogee of the centerpiece was reached in the Victorian age, with its cult of the hero and its hagiography of the great and the good. The greatest celebration of its artistic manifestations was the Centennial Exposition in Philadelphia in 1876. The William Cullen Bryant Vase exhibited by Tiffany & Company of New York was an allegorical extravaganza in honor of the poet and editor, an overstated 'Renaissance' urn circled with busts and vignettes of Bryant and overwhelmed with flowers and birds. It was produced at a cost of $5,000; this amount was raised by a subscription from the 'Friends of the Poet'.

But the undoubted star of the show was the Century Vase, a 2,000-ounce ode to the birthday of the republic, surmounted by the figure of America holding forth the olive branch and surrounded by allusions to the nation's history, achievements and vast natural wealth. Produced by Gorham & Company, under the direction of its designers George Wilkinson and Thomas J. Pairpoint, it was the exhibition's largest industrial art product.

It was fitting that Tiffany's and Gorham's creations should be the ones so praised and monumentalized, since it would be these two companies that would change the face of American silversmithing in the next decades, and whose fame would last for over a century.

SILVER: TEA- AND COFFEEPOTS, SERVICES AND CADDIES

With the fashion for drinking the then exotic beverages of coffee and tea came the demand for special vessels in which to serve them. Following their introduction in England, tea- and coffeepots both appeared in the colonies in the first quarter of the 18th century. The lines of both vessels were governed by the prevailing fashions of the area in which they were made – the 'bullet', or 'apple', shape was a particular favorite of Boston, while the 'pear' shape was more characteristic of New York. Early Philadelphia pieces seem to be in sympathy with the Boston fashion, although the paucity of contemporaneous Philadelphia examples makes it impossible to prove conclusively. In any case, there are always exceptions that throw all pronouncements into confusion: a matching coffeepot and sugar bowl by the New York goldsmith, Simeon Soumain (*c*1685–*c*1750), another Huguenot contemporary of Paul Revere, Sr, owned by the Museum of Fine Arts, Boston, could not be more severely elegant or less 'apple'-shaped.

Examples in the classic Queen Anne 'pear' shape, which continued in popularity for a longer period, are more frequent. In fact, it was this more curvaceous shape that developed into the greater

ABOVE: *Teapot by Jacob Hurd, Boston, c 1735–45. (Mabel Brady Garvan Collection, Yale University Art Gallery.)*

LEFT: *Coffeepot c 1760 by Myer Myers, New York. (The Saint Louis Art Museum.)*

number of Rococo 'Chippendale' tea- and coffeepot styles in evidence from 1750. Ebonized 'C'-curve handles curl from ornately finished silver fixtures, the spouts rise from a stylized bouquet of leaves, the gently pregnant Boston- or Philadelphia-style 'double-bellied' body rests on a low-molded pedestal foot, and the lid is topped by a pineapple, flame or swirled finial.

Tea caddies or canisters also came into use in this period. At first they were oblong with a cap cover, but in line with the changes in style that affected all silver, they changed with the fashion. Oval, circular and vase-shaped forms came and went in company with appropriate decoration. Caddies were never presented with the pot of brewed tea, but were kept separately in little shagreen, ivory or wooden boxes, often together with a covered sugar bowl. The tea was carefully measured out to be brewed and the canister replaced in its box, to be placed under lock and key.

ABOVE: *Six-piece mixed silver, copper and gilt tea and coffee service. (Christie's, New York.)*

By about 1790, the first tea and coffee services, with pot, sugar basin and cream jug, were appearing in America. In Boston, the Federal style paired a straight-sided or fluted oval teapot with a straight spout, small feet and bright-cut engraving, with a helmet-shaped creamer and sugar basin balanced on a single, square-bottomed foot. In contrast, Philadelphia preferred a more ovoid form for its pieces, replacing the incised decorative border of the Boston style with a pierced gallery and beading. In tea- and coffeepots, as in everything else, neo-Classical beading, reeding and fluting were succeeded by the opulence of the Empire style. The vase-shaped bodies again sported curving spouts, sometimes finishing in the head of a mythical beast. Lids were elongated, molded and often highly chased with acanthus leaves and other plant forms. It was a style that moved easily into the highly eclectic and overstated lavishness of the American Victorian age.

SILVER: ART SILVER

The last decades of the 19th century saw two major changes in the American silver establishment: the final emergence of designers trained in the American tradition, and the triumph of great companies over the independent craftsman. As late as 1853, *Harper's Monthly* felt constrained to observe that 'the time is not far off, we feel sure, when we shall have no need of foreign designers of our plate and jewelry.' The plain fact was, however, that they did.

While some second-generation craftsmen were already into their careers, and the design of American silver had shown the growth of a distinct national character, it remained that the major companies that had come into prominence with the mass-production of silver persistently looked toward Europe for their top expertise. The tradition of English and Continental silversmithing was a strong one, and the rise of the European-inspired Renaissance, Arts and Crafts and, lastly Art Nouveau movements would only serve to increase the respectful glances directed across the Atlantic. Gorham consistently brought over English designers to head its workshops, while Tiffany & Company was long under the influence of the German-trained Gustave Herter.

But by the late 1870s, Tiffany & Company could finally boast a native-born and -trained American, Edward C. Moore, as its chief designer and president. It may have helped, of course, that his father, John C. Moore, was head of the company that was incorporated with Tiffany's firm in 1868. It is not absolutely sure how much of the work in the Paris Exhibition of 1878 was actually his, and how much was the work of Japanese metalworkers, but the Oriental-style chased and inlaid ware produced under his direction received the attention of important international critics and identified Tiffany as a rising force in the silver world.

By the mid-19th century, a number of companies that would loom large in the annals of American silver had come into being. Gorham & Company, today a division of the Textron Corporation, was founded in Providence, Rhode Island, in 1831. Under the son, John, who took over the presidency from his father Jabez in 1847, the company opened additional offices in New York (1861), San Francisco and Chicago (both 1878). It was the first truly national silver company, one which could guarantee that the cutlery gracing the tables of New York's old money would be found at the dinner gatherings of the railroad magnates and Nob Hill new money in the West. Three years after Gorham opened its doors in Providence, Charles Louis Tiffany (*d*1902) founded the shop bearing his name in New York. In 1848, he extended his production to include jewelry which, together with the glassware designed by his son, Louis Comfort Tiffany, would become one of the best-received and lasting contributions to the Arts and Crafts and Art Nouveau movements.

Tiffany and Gorham both changed the face of silver design by their fascination with things Oriental. Both companies were particularly influenced by the arts of Japan, and produced articles in sterling silver and mixed metals that they termed

ABOVE: *Tiffany tea set, probably designed by Edward Moore. Silver, enamel, etched and gilded. Made in New York c 1888. (Metropolitan Museum of Art, New York.)*

LEFT: *Tiffany vase 'Magnolia', enameled silver; made in New York 1893. (Metropolitan Museum of Art, New York.)*

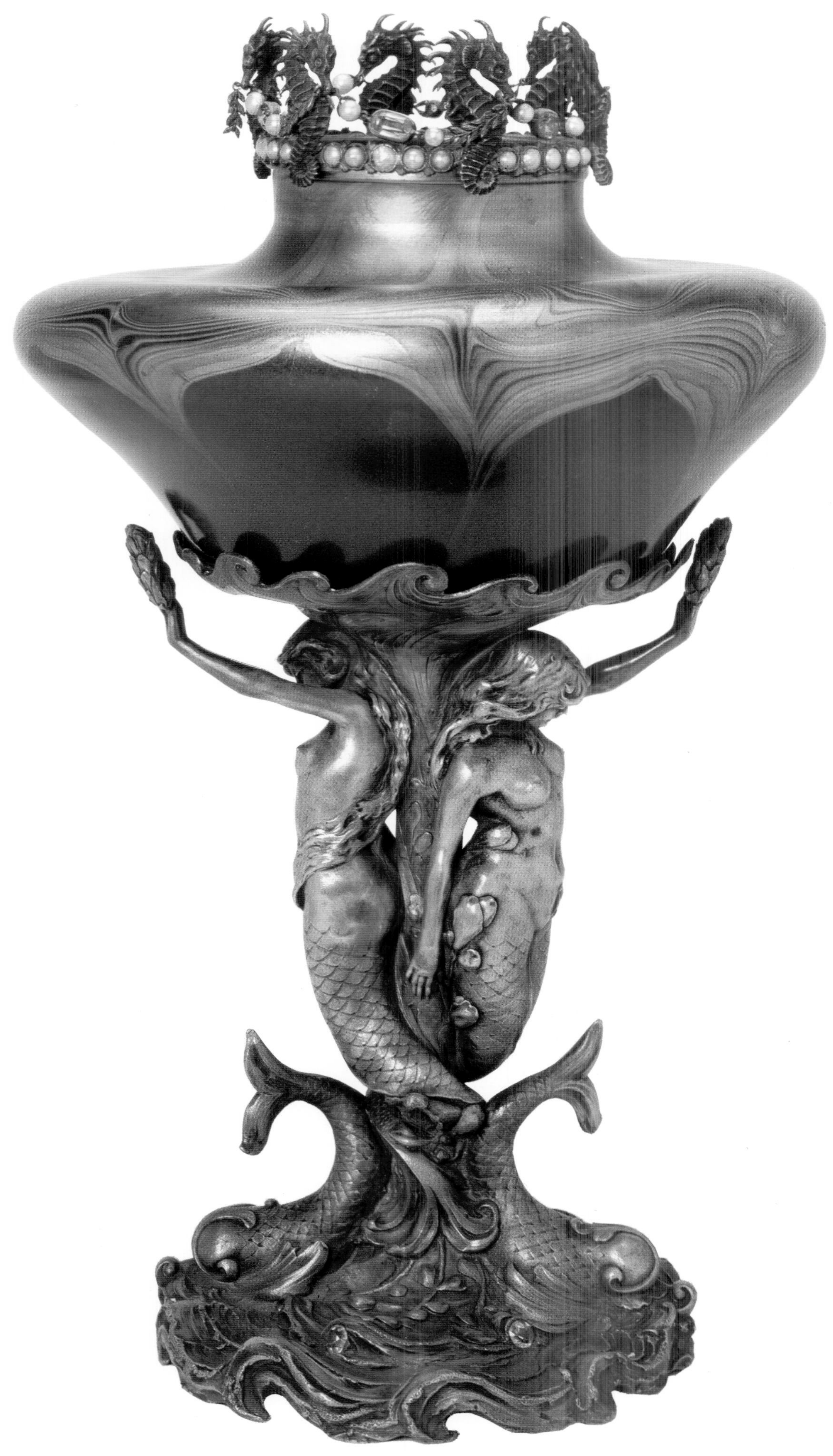

'Japanese style.' The surface would either be silver – with silver, gold and copper applied as flora and fauna – or a copper ground with the silver applied. Favorite motifs included cranes, dragonflies, crabs, dragons, bulrushes and irises, with the occasional human figure included for good measure.

Tiffany had already opened a shop on London's Regent Street in 1868, for Tiffany and Moore realized that acceptance abroad would guarantee success at home. The Gold Medal at the Paris Exhibition in 1878 put the imprimatur on their wares; soon English customers were buying in large numbers and English designers – not only of silver – were taking inspiration from the pieces. The wave of Japanese fashion, both celebrated and lampooned by Gilbert & Sullivan in *The Mikado*, owed much of its enormous vitality to the initial impetus delivered by the Americans.

ABOVE: *Tiffany stone-set silver vase, designed for the Paris Exposition of 1900. (Christie's, New York.)*

LEFT: *An iridescent glass vase on silver stand, by Tiffany, 1897. (Sotheby's, New York.)*

The other large companies that were operating by the 1870s and 1880s included the Whiting Manufacturing Company of North Attleboro, Massachusetts; Samuel Kirk & Sons of Baltimore (already in business in the 1840s); Wood & Hughes, New York; Dominick & Haff, New York; International Silver Company in Meriden, Connecticut (founded in 1852 as the Meriden Brittania Company); and Reed & Barton in Taunton, Massachusetts – the latter, like Gorham, still a name to be reckoned with in modern sterling. Although as late as the 1920s Louis Comfort Tiffany could still complain that 'the average American would rather bring back poor and thoroughly artistic work from abroad than purchase domestic art in his own country', happily his words applied much less to the silver and jewelry side of the family firm than to his own marvelous glassware.

C H A P T E R F O U R

OTHER METALWORK

From copper kettles to Navajo necklaces: practical pieces of history and items collected for art's sake.

ABOVE: *Navajo jewelry of the early 1900s. (Jerry Jacka Photography/Heard Museum, Phoenix.)*

18th- AND 19th-CENTURY PEWTER

Pewter, widely made in Europe since medieval times, has proved a popular material for useful wares. In America, however, the alloy boasts a far shorter history. The earliest record of a working pewterer refers to one Richard Graves, a master craftsman who opened a shop in Salem, Massachusetts, in 1635. Nine other pewterers were registered in Boston, New York and Philadelphia before 1750, but even these limited numbers are misleading. Outside of a spoon found in excavations at Jamestown, Virginia, and embossed with the maker's mark of Joseph Copeland of Chuckatuck and Jamestown (who worked from *c*1675 to 1691), the earliest definitely attributable piece dates from *c*1725, and any pewter dating from before 1750 is exceedingly rare. Indeed, even pieces that can be ascribed with certainty as pre-Revolutionary are unusual. The evidence points to the fact that the vast majority of these registered pewterers were not, in fact, makers but repairers and importers. The extreme rarity of this early American ware makes it highly attractive to wealthy collectors, and pieces that appear at auction consistently bring in international record prices.

Although most pewter in the colonies seems to have been imported, the basis for American production slowly built up. Since it was much hardier than crockery or glass, it was the obvious choice for the average householder and the pioneers who slowly penetrated the hinterland. Although America was lacking in tin resources, and England had imposed a prohibitive tax on raw imported tin, the newly émigré English craftsmen in the colonies saw their opportunity in reworking the old pewter that came their way through exchange.

The real history of American pewter begins around 1750 and extends to the mid-19th century, during which time the most proficient craftsmen developed their own uniquely American style. Among the great names at work in the second half of the 18th century whose marked pieces command respect and high prices are Francis and Frederick Bassett of New York; William and Cornelius Bradford of New York and Philadelphia; Joseph and Thomas Danforth II of Middletown, Connecticut; Benjamin Day of Newport, Connecticut and Jamestown, Massachusetts; Simon Edgell of Philadelphia; Gershom Jones of Providence; Michael Lee of Taunton, Massachusetts; Henry Will of New York and Albany; William Will of Philadelphia, and Peter Young of Albany.

Between 1750 and 1820 pewter styles changed little; English influence remained uppermost, although it was given a good run for its money in the early days by the modifying impact of Continentally trained artisans. The English-trained pewterers excelled in their hammerwork, producing brilliant effects on the metal's surface through innumerable

ABOVE: *Chanticleer weathervane, c 1880, of an unknown metal, probably copper. (American Folk Art.)*

LEFT: *Pewter inkstand or writing box by Henry Will, c 1761–93. The inkstand is a container for pens, sand and wafers used in letter writing. Very few pewter inkstands have survived. (The Brooklyn Museum Collection.)*

ABOVE: *Cast-iron horse weathervane in old mustard paint, from the mid 19th century. (Thomas K. Woodward Antiques, New York.)*

tiny indentations. In addition, their fluid pierced work – seen to its best effect on porringer handles – contrasted with the solid tab handles with incised decoration made by European-influenced craftsmen.

Since they could not compete with the variety of forms and styles imported from England – the cost of molds was too high – American workers concentrated on simple designs: smooth-rimmed and single reed plates, clean 'Federal style' coffeepots and tankards. The Rococo style never took hold in American pewter. By the 1820s the firm of Reed & Barton was manufacturing pewter domestic ware on a large scale, and by 1825 Britannia ware – a spun and cold-molded variation on pewter – had begun mass-production at the firm of Hiram Yale in Wallingford, Connecticut. For the next 25 to 30 years pewterers attempted to adapt the changing fashions of silver to pewter, but with diminishing success. After 1850 interest in collectible American pewter is relatively limited.

Early American pewter is notorious for its cavalier use of marks, which often aped those of English makers and attempted to lead the unwary into believing the item was imported or of better quality (either an 'X' for high-quality pewter, or 'hallmarks' for silver) than it actually was. The use of the Federal eagle became commonplace in touchmarks in post-Revolutionary days, sometimes surrounded by stars indicating the number of states – a useful dating device. But after 1800, maker's marks became much less florid, usually a simple name or initials in a frame, if it was signed at all. The later, post-1820 pieces often demand specialist knowledge to date or attribute with any great accuracy.

FACING PAGE: *Liberty with flag iron weathervane c 1880. (American Folk Art.)*

OTHER METALS: COPPER, TIN, BRASS AND IRON

An enormous number and variety of household, agricultural and architectural articles were made of brass, copper, iron and tin, from the days of the earliest colonists onward, and today these vintage objects form one of the largest categories for the collector. Since few pieces are signed, their interest lies in their age and aesthetic attraction. At the one end are the wonderfully forged iron or sheet-copper weather vanes, the eipitome of the metalworker's art, which are rare and highly expensive when found. At the other are the many homely and fairly easily discovered items of domestic and farmyard use, much loved by interior decorators but highly collectible in their own right as well. While the rarity of the former means that 19th-century and even exceptional 20th-century pieces are much sought-after by the collector, the more common wrought-iron and brass utensils found in antiques shops and private collections may easily date back to the 18th and, in the case of iron, even the 17th centuries.

ABOVE: *Deer weathervane made of iron, c 1870. (American Folk Art.)*

RIGHT: *Iron bull weathervane by S. Howard c 1850. (American Folk Art.)*

Copper and iron were much favored for outdoor uses – copper for its relative lightness and resistance to rust; iron for its weight and durability. Both were employed to make weather vanes. The earliest were made of two pieces of sheet copper hammered out on a plank, then soldered together over a mount to give a figure in low relief. Later, in the 19th century, the copper was molded in iron casts, resulting in highly detailed examples. They were produced by factories such as Cushing & White of Waltham, Massachusetts, and occasionally signed. Wrought-iron vanes came into vogue in the early 19th century, preferred in many cases for the individuality that the working of the metal allowed the forger to exhibit. Cast-iron pieces invaded – and dominated – the market by 1860.

By the mid-19th century small factories and blacksmiths were turning out any number of stock patterns, but there were also those farmers and landowners who demanded their own unique totems. The combination has given museums and collections a rich parade of figures human, animal and other: from Indians and hunters, to witches-on-broomsticks and sulkies-with-drivers; from the much-loved running horses and crowing cocks, to foxes and the more pedestrian relatives of the beautiful gold-leaf grasshopper on Boston's Faneuil Hall. Even ships and locomotives appeared as weather-vane motifs.

Humbler uses for metal abounded. Copper had been used in Great Britain to make water and teakettles since the mid-18th century, and colonial coppersmiths took up the manufacture with avidity. But they added a certain flair to their designs, producing a version with a characteristic flared gooseneck spout and hinged handle. These remained popular into the 19th century, continuing in production even when their primacy was replaced by the new spun-brass kettles, made in numbers from the mid-19th century. Occasional examples of both types are signed or stamped with a maker's name and town, usually in New York or Pennsylvania.

Pounded sheet brass and copper were used to outfit 18th- and 19th-century kitchens and hearths. Measures, scales, pots and pans, wood holders, foot and bed warmers, chestnut roasters, funnels, fish kettles, trivets, lamp stands and oil-lamp fillers are among the most common items found today. Brass casting came to the colonies by the 1720s, although at first only small items like buttons and drawer handles and pulls were produced by this method. But by the late 18th century, the craft had become established. Wealthier homes could boast cast-brass 'Chippendale' andirons with lemon, urn or ball finials, while the austere steepled churches so characteristic of New England were endowed with elegant branched brass chandeliers. Bootjacks, door knockers, doorstops, paperweights and countless other domestic objects followed throughout the 19th century. However, cast-brass objects are still produced in their thousands today using antique-style molds, and it is virtually impossible for the non-specialist to distinguish the old from the newly minted. A thorough grounding in period casting techniques, together with the opportunity to compare a wide variety of items, is required (an option open mainly to experienced dealers and long-time collectors).

ABOVE: *Tin lantern, c 1800–50. Unidentified maker, probably from New York, Pennsylvania or New England. Pierced tinplate with wire, horn and remains of paint. (Abby Aldrich Rockefeller, American Folk Art Center.)*

From the earliest days of settlement, however, the main bulk of everyday utensils was made from plain, unvarnished tin and wrought iron. The former, although rendered relatively costly by import duties for the sheet metal, was used for lightweight storage boxes for candles and flints, as well as for wall sconces and lanterns, funnels, tea- and coffeepots, and candle forms (candles being the handiwork of the housewife in settlers' and later, pioneer, households). Iron was heavier and more expensive, but it was indispensible to homes

of ordinary folk. The blacksmith was among the most common trades noted in early records, and although the first colonial craftsmen had to import their raw material, it was not long before iron was being smelted on this side of the Atlantic. After an ill-fated attempt in 1622 to set up a furnace at Falling Creek, Virginia (the site fell victim to an Indian massacre), it was several years before another was successfully opened. But by the 1680s Massachusetts had at least one furnace producing pig iron, and by the 1750s, several were exporting iron to Great Britain. Both hand-wrought iron and cast iron were fashioned from this domestic product.

The majority of iron items found in public and private collections today date from the mid-18th century and later. For kitchen and chimney use, pothooks, cranes, toasters, trivets, spits and fire irons were forged by local blacksmiths, while three-footed skillets, cauldrons, andirons and firebacks were cast in foundries. Hinges, catches, latches, hasps and foot scrapers form another category of interest – one that has a greater chance of attribution and dating than that of probably any other iron fixtures. Parochial styles and designs betray the regions where the items were made; the difference between the simplicity of a Massachusetts hinge and the foliate turns of a Pennsylvania German example are obvious cases in point. In addition, farm and trade implements often combine two or more materials – such as wood, iron and brass – extending the collector's horizon.

OTHER METALWORK: TOLEWARE AND PENNSYLVANIA DUTCH METALWARE

Because the Pennsylvania Dutch were so fond of bright colors and stenciled and painted designs on their furniture, it was long assumed that much of the decorated and japanned tinware that was popular during the early to mid-19th century was from their hands. However, it now seems that this was a sweeping attribution and that much, if not most, of the lacquered tinware found in collections today had its origins up the coast in the tin centres of New England. Certainly the naïve charm of these items would have appealed as much to the Amish housewife as to her country sisters, and the fact that the tinwares were distributed by peddlers would have made their spread to a wide and varied public an obvious corollary. Certainly the local tinsmiths of 19th-century Pennsylvania produced canisters, teapots, caddies and apple baskets to delight their own folk, replicating many of the themes and colors that appear on their furniture; but the quantity is much restricted when compared to the output of the Northeastern settlements.

ABOVE: *Early 19th-century Scotch broiler. The easel leg on back adjusts the angle of meat facing fire. (Pat Guthman Antiques.)*

TOP: *17th-century bronze cooking pot. (Pat Guthman Antiques.)*

FACING PAGE: *Tin lantern, made in New Mexico c 1830. (The American Museum in Britain.)*

Tin was an expensive and rare commodity to the colonist, since all supplies came from England, which levied severe import duties. After the Revolution the supply from the mother country resumed, at somewhat better prices. At about the same time, the fashion for japanning was also introduced. This provided a stimulus to the tin centers, which were primarily located in the Connecticut River Valley. In its simplest practice, japanned tin plate – or toleware, as it is more often called in the United States, after the highly finished products of the

RIGHT: *Pair of brass andirons, late 18th century. Each with spiral flame and faceted diamond finial above a spiral baluster-shaped shaft over a plinth, on spurred-arched legs with ball-and-claw feet. (Christie's, New York.)*

BELOW: *Toleware coffee pot, early 19th century, Massachusetts. (The American Museum in Britain.)*

18th-century French makers – is made by coating sheet-tin articles with asphaltum varnish, heating them to affix the paint and then decorating them. But unlike the sophisticated products of Usk and Pontypool in Great Britain and France's Parisian factories, those of late 18th- and 19th-century America remained resolutely countrified and simple – no gold leaf or painterly effects for the American rustics.

The credit for founding the American japanning business is often given to the Pattison family. The two Irish-born brothers, William and Edward, received their training in England and came to settle in what is today Berlin, Connecticut. They began as simple tinsmiths in the 1740s, turning out sheet-tin trays, boxes of all sizes and uses, and tea caddies and teapots. But with the resumption of business after the war, the apprentices trained by the Pattisons took up the tin trade and enhanced it with the inclusion of the newly imported japanning, establishing several local outlets as well as others around and beyond Berlin. Chief among their students was Oliver Buckley, who produced

ABOVE: *Toleware basket made in Pennsylvania in the 19th century. (The American Museum in Britain.)*

gay freehand designs, incorporating naïvely stylized flowers and leaves, together with round spots of orange color and sprouting or encircling brush-strokes in paler hues. Generally, the complete design is round in shape, often with a running border in red, green and/or black on a white background along the top edge or foot of the piece.

Other freehand painters include the itinerant Oliver Filley, who began his tin-making, decorating and selling business in Vermont, but branched out to include outlets in Philadelphia, Lansingburgh, New York, and Bloomfield, Connecticut, in the heart of the tin centers; and the Butlers of East Greenville, New York, whose artists numbered Ann, Minerva and Marilla, daughters of tinsmith Aaron Butler. By the third decade of the 19th century, most of the free-painters were women, who used their craft to supplement their income or assisted their husbands or fathers, who were often in the tin-working trade.

A new technique came into prominence around 1825 – stenciling. It enabled far greater output than even the quick brushstrokes of the hand-painters. The defter application of paint over the black allowed the colors to glow yellow, green, red, white and brown. The stenciling technique was also centered around Berlin, though it again spread beyond it. Stenciled objects can easily be distinguished from the hand-painted by the clear demarcation of the pattern and the evenness of the paint application.

After 1850, the fashion for tole work gradually declined, although japanned toys and papier-mâché cases, boxes and furniture were produced in a limited quantity, but never in the numbers they enjoyed in Great Britain and on the Continent.

OTHER METALWORK: NAVAJO AND INDIAN JEWELRY

Southwestern Indian jewelry has been available to the non-Indian collector for roughly the past 90 years. Before that time, the Indians bartered the handmade bracelets, earrings, rings and necklaces with a few licensed traders in return for saddles, cloth, tools and other necessary items. Occasionally,

ABOVE: *This range of Indian jewelry varies in style from a highly contemporary gold necklace (left) to traditional Navajo, Zuni and Santo Domingo pieces. (Jerry Jacka Photography/Heard Museum, Phoenix.)*

these early bartered and pawned pieces have found their way into private hands. For the most part, however, it was not until the arrival of the Santa Fe Railroad – and with it the trading posts administered by the Harvey Company – that the public at large was exposed to this uniquely American artistic idiom. Even so, it remained a sleeping craft, relatively unexploited in terms of mass-production and imitation, until the late 1960s. Then, inspired by the hippies, the fad for all things ethnic took flight. The flower children made Santa Fe their provincial capital, attracting makers of 'handicrafts' even less scrupulous than themselves. The days of quality workmanship were numbered. The consequence of all this, however, is that what is in real terms a recently developed craft was given the time to evolve into a truly indigenous art form, one whose finest pieces deserve the high prices they now command.

The main focus of collectors' interest has always been the jewelry of the Navajo – the Revere family, if you like, of the Golden West. The first Southwestern American Indian tribe to work silver – probably beginning around 1870 – they have always remained, first and foremost, *silversmiths.* Inspired and, perhaps, taught by the Mexican artisans with whom they came into contact (it seems they traded their horses for learning the skill), the early Indian smiths showed an uncanny gift for adapting both Mexican and Spanish engraving motifs to their roughly worked metal. Although gravely restricted by a lack of tools, they nevertheless managed to produce a simple catalog of designs simply by using files and pipe stamps. By the 1880s they were employing the cold chisel, awl and punch, and by the late 1880s they were designing their own stamps. When stamping became the preferred method of decoration, the Navajo entered their finest hour, displaying their technical brilliance in complex designs on both cast and hammered pieces.

Indian jewelers from the 1870s to 1890s used melted American silver coins, then switched to pesos until the 1900s. Thereafter they used silver slugs manufactured for the purpose and continued to use them until the 1940s (although by this time sheet silver had been introduced). Many older pieces were melted down and the silver combined with the newer sheets or the slugs – so it is virtually

Above: *Modern Navajo jewelry by Thomas Singer. Such modern work retains many of the motifs of traditional Navajo work. (Jerry Jacka Photography.)*

impossible to date a piece merely from the type of silver used. A thorough knowledge of the tools employed, the designs popular in particular periods, and even the type and treatment of stones is necessary to ascribe a date or specific place of origin to a piece.

Although most people associate turquoise with Navajo jewelry, inset stones did not become common until around 1900. Initially it was members of the Zuni tribe who were the stoneworkers, and to this day they retain the laurels as the premier jewelers among the American Indians. While the Navajo were busy learning silver-working, the Zuni were refining their stone-setting techniques, and by the 1920s the two tribes had exchanged much knowledge. However, while the Navajo would confine their use of turquoise or moonstone to a few large stones – nothing ever more extravagant than a sunburst – concentrating rather on the finesse of the surrounding design, the Zuni explored inlay and channel work in turquoise, shell and colored stones, as well as cluster and row-work settings of polished turquoise. The total effect of a Zuni design is one of delicacy – a web pattern of blue or an intricate map of desert geology – while, in contrast, that of the Navajo is strength and singleness of purpose.

Chief among the Navajo items are *conchas*, oval or round pieces of wrought silver made to be worn on a leather belt; 'squash blossom' necklaces, named for the elongated pomegranates pendent around the circumference; *najas*, crescent moons used as brooches and as pendants on necklaces; earrings, bracelets and rings. In all these pieces it is the working and the tooling of the silver that raises them from the ordinary to the highly collectible. In Zuni jewelry, bracelets, brooches and rings play a far greater part, and the amount of silver used may be minimal. In both forms of jewelry, while the color and placement of the stones obviously play a part in the aesthetic effect of the pieces, the actual fineness and worth of the stones themselves are of secondary importance to the collector. Indeed, because these are folk pieces, worked by a people without much money or many resources, the attraction of the jewelry lies in its artistic expression, not in the intrinsic value of their materials.

C H A P T E R F I V E

GLASS

The rich tradition of American glassmaking sets the scene for the work of Tiffany and others.

ABOVE: *Glass vase from the Bakewell plant, Pittsburgh, Pennsylvania. Blown from clear lead glass; the foot was made separately. (The American Museum in Britain.)*

FREE-BLOWN GLASS

The documented history of glassware in the United States is short – a mere 250 years – but significant. In that relatively limited time, America has managed to contribute substantially to both the art and the technological development of the craft.

There is reference to glassmaking in the Jamestown, Virginia, settlement as early as 1609, but little is known of the following century's production. It would seem that there was small-scale production of bottles and drinking vessels in Virginia, the Massachusetts Bay Colony and New Amsterdam (later New York), but for the most part the colonists survived on utensils of horn, pewter and earthenware, with cherished pieces of imported English or Continental silver or glass occasionally found in richer homes. Save for some fragments of glass excavated at the Jamestown site and attributed to local workmanship, no piece of American glass survives that can confidently be dated pre-1740.

During the third quarter of the 18th century, some 10 factories began production in the colonies, producing mainly utilitarian wares such as bottles and window-glass. This was both politically sound – since colonial production of tableware was forbidden by royal edict – and economically expedient. Indeed, despite the increasingly sophisticated wares turned out in the followng 100 years, these two items – particularly green bottle glass – would continue to be the mainstay of American glasshouses, subsidizing the more creative pieces risked by commercially minded management. Those factories that did not assume this conservative attitude often went bankrupt.

The type of glass produced by these early glasshouses is known collectively as South Jersey glass, in honor of the first and most famous area producing it. The Wistarburg glasshouse (*c*1739–80) in Salem County, southern New Jersey, was the initial effort of Caspar Wistar (1696–1752), a German immigrant, who had no qualifications as a glassmaker, being described as a 'brass button-maker' in contemporary documents. He nevertheless determined that there the demand for locally produced glass justified breaking the royal ban. By the 1740s his enterprise was turning out free-blown jugs, pitchers, dishes and flasks in sturdy bottle glass, in addition to the usual bread-and-butter work of windows and bottles. Soon other factories were following his lead, including the Glass House Company of New York, with works in New York (*c*1752–75) and New Windsor, as well as in Germantown, near Boston (*c*1753–67).

The style and techniques spread further afield, to the Midwest and even back to England, where the tradition carried on in the works of the Nailsea and Birmingham factories. In the United States, it continued until the mid-19th century. Although Wistar's son failed to extend his father's success and the factory closed down in 1780, one of his apprentices, Jacob Stanger, in partnership with his brother, opened the Glassboro Works in Gloucester County, New Jersey, in 1781. This glasshouse, and the later Harmony glassworks founded by the brothers in 1813, brought the South Jersey tradition well and truly into the 19th century.

ABOVE: *Late 18th-century engraved flip glass with tulip design. (The American Museum in Britain.)*

Historians tend to divide South Jersey-style free-blown pieces into two eras: early South Jersey glass and post-1825. Although no pieces can definitely be ascribed to Wistar's factory, those known to be of the early period, when not plain, are distinguished by their bold applied decoration, tooled into ornamentation. Prunts, threading and crimping were succeeded by gadrooning, swagging and, in the 19th century, the signature device of the South Jersey style, the lily pad. This was accomplished by a superimposed layer of hot glass, trailed and looped. Pieces from the South Jersey region range from light aquamarine through yellow-green; those from New York are in a brighter aquamarine, as well as a few examples in amber, green or yellow,

R·W

ABOVE LEFT: *'Trisler' goblet, 1793, of colorless glass, blown and engraved. From New Bremen Glass. (Corning Museum of Glass.)*

ABOVE RIGHT: *Colorless non-lead glass tumbler, blown and engraved with initials 'GMR'. Made c 1790–95 by New Bremen Glass. (Corning Museums of Glass.)*

FACING PAGE: *(Left to right) blown and engraved tumbler, 1751; blown wine bottle c 1745–55; blown and tooled taperstick c 1739–76; blown and tooled cream basket c 1739–76. (Corning Museum of Glass.)*

LEFT: *Tumbler with cover in the form of a glass sphere. (The American Museum in Britain.)*

ABOVE: *Free-blown aquamarine glass bowl with lily pad decoration. Made by Redford Crown Glass Works 1831–50. (Hirschl and Adler Galleries, New York.)*

while New England versions occur most often in amber or olive green.

After 1840 some true blue pieces are also seen. Some of the most elaborate covered sugar bowls are topped by a bird, either chicken, swan, peacock or indeterminate fowl; these are collectively known as 'swan finials.' Post-1820 pieces from the New Jersey region were sometimes decorated by 'lopping and dragging' in white over a light aquamarine or other transluscent base; even later the base might be of a darker glass. While blowers in New York, New Jersey and New England remained true to traditional forms of decoration, those in the Midwest began to experiment with pattern-molding, decorating their wares with ribbing, 'popcorn' swirls and widely expanded diamonds.

While the name of Henry William 'Baron' Stiegel (1729–85) is almost synonymous with early pattern-molded ware, he is also important for the quality of the few engraved and enameled free-blown pieces that survive from the later part of his productive life. Although he opened his first factory in 1763, he only began to market enameled items in 1772, during the last two to three years before bankruptcy claimed his businesses. The clear glass for which he became so famous was deftly painted in enameled colors with patterns common to, or reminiscent of, those fashionable on the Continent, particularly Germany. Hearts, flowers and birds, arabesques and swirls decorate his charming glasses, pitchers and bottles, doubtless designed by his Manheim glasshouses to appeal to the nearby Pennsylvania German market.

Even more elegant were the works of the New Bremen Glass Manufactory (1785–95) near Frederick, Maryland, founded by John Frederick Amelung. His fine, lead-free glass was wheel-engraved in the richest Continental fashion and further embellished with applied and tooled decoration, including metalwork and occasional gilding and enameling. The pieces that have been attributed to (or signed by) him are mainly presentation pieces – usually goblets or covered tumblers – the most famous being the wonderful *Tobias and the Angel*, dated 1781 and dedicated to a member of the Amelung family, and the *Bremen Pokal*, made and engraved in 1788 and sent to Germany to demonstrate the factory's skill.

RIGHT: *'Stenger' flask, 1792, from New Bremen Glass; blown and engraved. (Corning Museum of Glass.)*

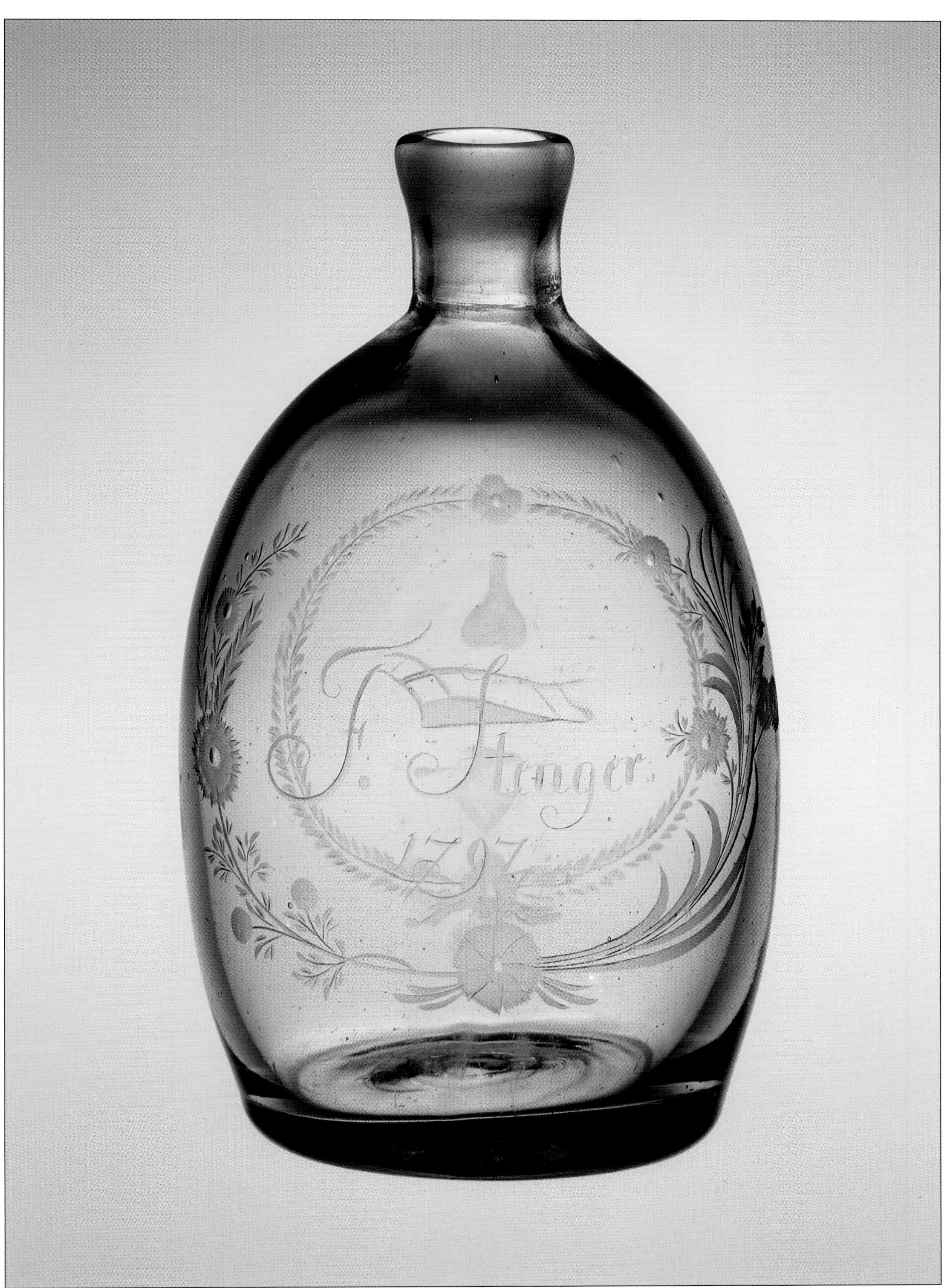
F. Stenger
1797

Top left: *Sugar bowl with cover with chicken finial,* c *1800. Bowl made in southern New Jersey, possibly Milford; cover southern New Jersey. (Corning Museum of Glass.)*

Far left: *Salt,* c *1788–1795; probably New Bremen Glass. Transparent and blue glass; blown and pattern-molded. (Corning Museum of Glass.)*

Left: *Blown wine glass* c *1800–20. Colorless glass with mottled purple stain. (Wendt Vornees Collection, Corning Museum of Glass.)*

Top right: *The valor cup, 1941; Steuben Glass Inc. Colorless lead glass; blown and engraved. (Corning Museum of Glass.)*

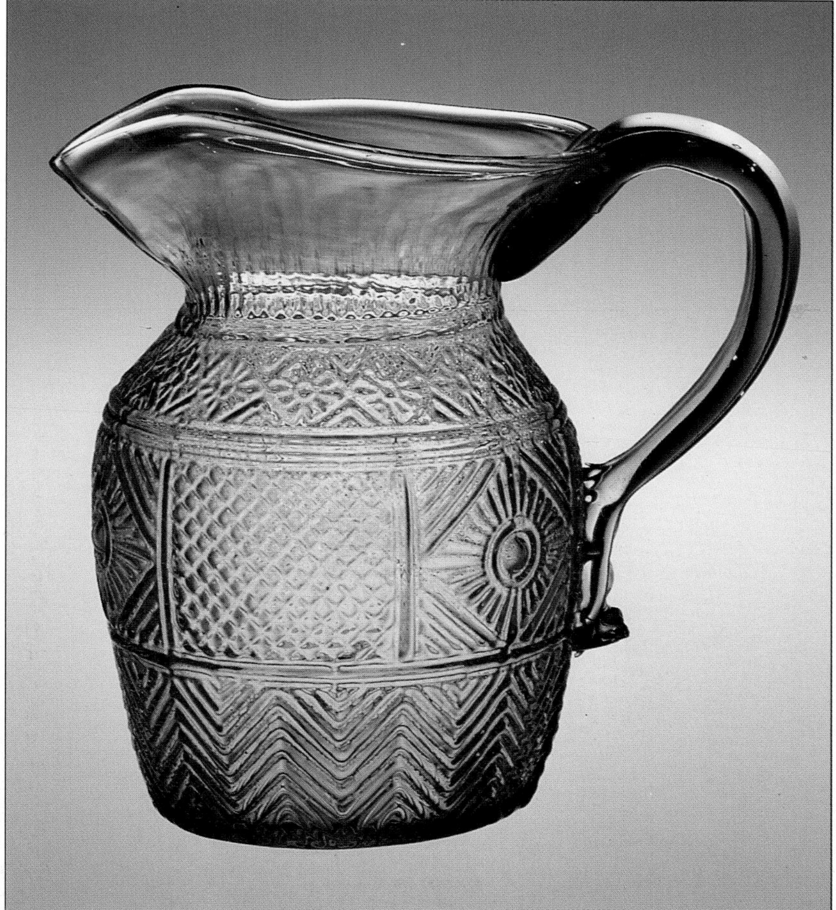

ABOVE: *Pair of tumblers, c 1770–1800. Formerly thought to be Steigel but now thought to be Germanic, indicating the similarities in style. Colorless non-lead glass, blown and enameled. (Corning Museum of Glass.)*

LEFT: *Pitcher, c 1825–40 by the Boston and Sandwich Glass Company. Colorless lead glass; mold-blown. (Corning Museum of Glass.)*

ABOVE: *Pocket bottle c 1765–1774; attributed to American Flint Glass. Transparent amethyst glass; pattern-molded and blown. (Corning Museum of Glass.)*

GLASS: 18th- AND 19th-CENTURY BLOWN AND MOLDED GLASS

Only two pre-Revolutionary businesses seem to have truly specialized in tableware – Henry William Stiegel's second Manheim factory and the Philadelphia Glass Works, founded in Kensington in 1771 – both, notably, in Pennsylvania. Each purported to be the first flint-glass (otherwise called lead glass) manufacturer in the country, and certainly Stiegel's uncolored glass was finer than most early efforts. But he is remembered today primarily as the founder of the second great tradition of American glass, following in the wake of South Jersey's free-blown works: 'Stiegel' or pattern-molded glass.

An immigrant from Cologne who was funded by his father-in-law to set himself up as a manufacturer, Stiegel opened his first glasshouse in Elizabeth Furnace, Pennsylvania, in 1763. In 1765 he opened another, at Manheim, and then a third in 1769 in the same place, all working simultaneously. All three factories employed some English workers, but the majority were German, and this preference shows in the styling of the factory's free-blown pieces. It was at the last factory that Stiegel finally took the plunge into channeling the major part of his flint glass and colored glass production – mainly blues, greens and amethysts – into pattern molds.

As Stiegel's workers tended to copy German and Continental designs in engraved and enameled pieces, so they adapted their molded glasswares to the English taste that prevailed in this type of decoration. In many cases it is a matter of expert opinion whether a piece of glass is American or English, so well did the Manheim craftsmen imitate the ribbing, fluting and diamond patterns of the Bristol glass houses popular in fashionable English and colonial circles. But Stiegel was a creative artist, not merely a cipher for foreign ideas, and he added patterns of his own to the repertoire – such as the diamond-in-hexagon and the daisy-in-square – neither of which has yet been matched to any contemporary British glass. But Stiegel's business acumen did not match his artistic strength, and the factory went under in 1774.

The Philadelphia Glass Works in Kensington lasted until just after the outbreak of the Revolu-

RIGHT: *Candlestick of non-lead glass, blown and pattern-molded; made c 1739–76, possibly by the Wistarburgh Glassworks. (Corning Museum of Glass.)*

tion – 1777 – and was sold in a run-down state. It had offered an incredible variety of items, ranging from decanters to goblets and glasses, from candlesticks and sweetmeat dishes to inkwells and every size and shape of lamp, from salt cellars and tobacco pipes to urinals. But the War of Independence spelled disaster for domestically produced consumer goods, and such factories did not resurface until the war was officially ended and the Constitution signed.

ABOVE: *Sugar bowl of sapphire-blue glass, attributed to Henry William Stiegel; made c 1765–74. (Brooklyn Museum, Dick S. Ramsay Fund.)*

Between 1783 and 1824 some 94 glasshouses set up in business, but the casualty rate was enormous. Notable among the – at least initial – successes were the Pittsburgh Glass Works (1797), with America's first coal furnace; Albert Gallatin's Glass Works in New Geneva, Pennsylvania (1798); John Bakewell of Pittsburgh (1809), who began in pattern-molded glass but would gain his greatest fame in production of the newfangled pressed glass; the New England Glass Company in Cambridge, Massachusetts (1818); and in New York the Fisher Brothers' Bloomingdale Flint Glass Works (1822) and the Brooklyn Flint Glass Works (1823), which gained the prize for the best flint-glass metal in London's Great Exhibition in 1851.

But all the new ventures had to struggle grimly for survival, since the newly independent American market was flooded with glasswares from England and Germany. It was not until 1824 that the American government was able to guarantee some protection for the troubled industry by imposing a tariff on the highly competitive foreign glass, followed by larger duties in 1828 and 1832. Ninety new glassworks were erected between 1825 and 1850, the majority beginning in patterned flint glass. As much as one-third of these enterprises opened

numerically. The term is used to cover glassware made with two- or four-piece molds as well, although the three-piece was the most usual. The technique, though not as widespread as pattern-molding, was gaining in distinction as a primarily American development when both methods were superseded by the meteoric rise of pressed glass around 1835.

GLASS: PICTORIAL, COMMEMORATIVE AND HISTORICAL FLASKS

As mentioned before, most glasshouses could not have survived as suppliers merely of tableware. Their mainstay was the production of window glass and bottles, straightforward items required by merchants and householders, rich and poor. The invention of the piece-mold, however, suggested to more commercially minded glasshouses that even something as utilitarian as a bottle could be made more distinctive and attractive to buyers. The result was a rash of pictorial bottles and flasks celebrating people, places and events. As a generic group their popularity lasted from about 1815 to 1870, although even today we can see their legacy in the 'Collec-

ABOVE: *Covered sugar bowl, c 1820–35, probably New England. Colorless glass; pattern-molded and blown. (Corning Museum of Glass.)*

RIGHT: *Decanter and stopper, c 1825–35, attributed to Boston and Sandwich Glass Works, Massachusetts. Colorless glass. (Corning Museum of Glass.)*

FACING PAGE: *Covered sugar bowl attributed to American Flint Glass. Made c 1769–74; dark blue lead glass, blown and pattern-molded.*

in the burgeoning Midwest, where the settlers did not have the money or opportunity to import from abroad.

Cut glass was still the glass of choice to the rich who could afford it, and around 1815 some of these factories began to experiment with, and then market, blown three-mold glass as a low-cost approximation. While the faceting and patterns were not as sharp as on pattern-molded glass, and the imprint of the mold was often visible, the structure of the mold allowed an exterior-interior correspondence more like that of real cut glass and the available designs were more varied than those allowed by pattern-mold production; most imitated faithfully those designs common to Irish and English cut glass. The patterns are today classified as arch, baroque and geometric, with the latter dominating

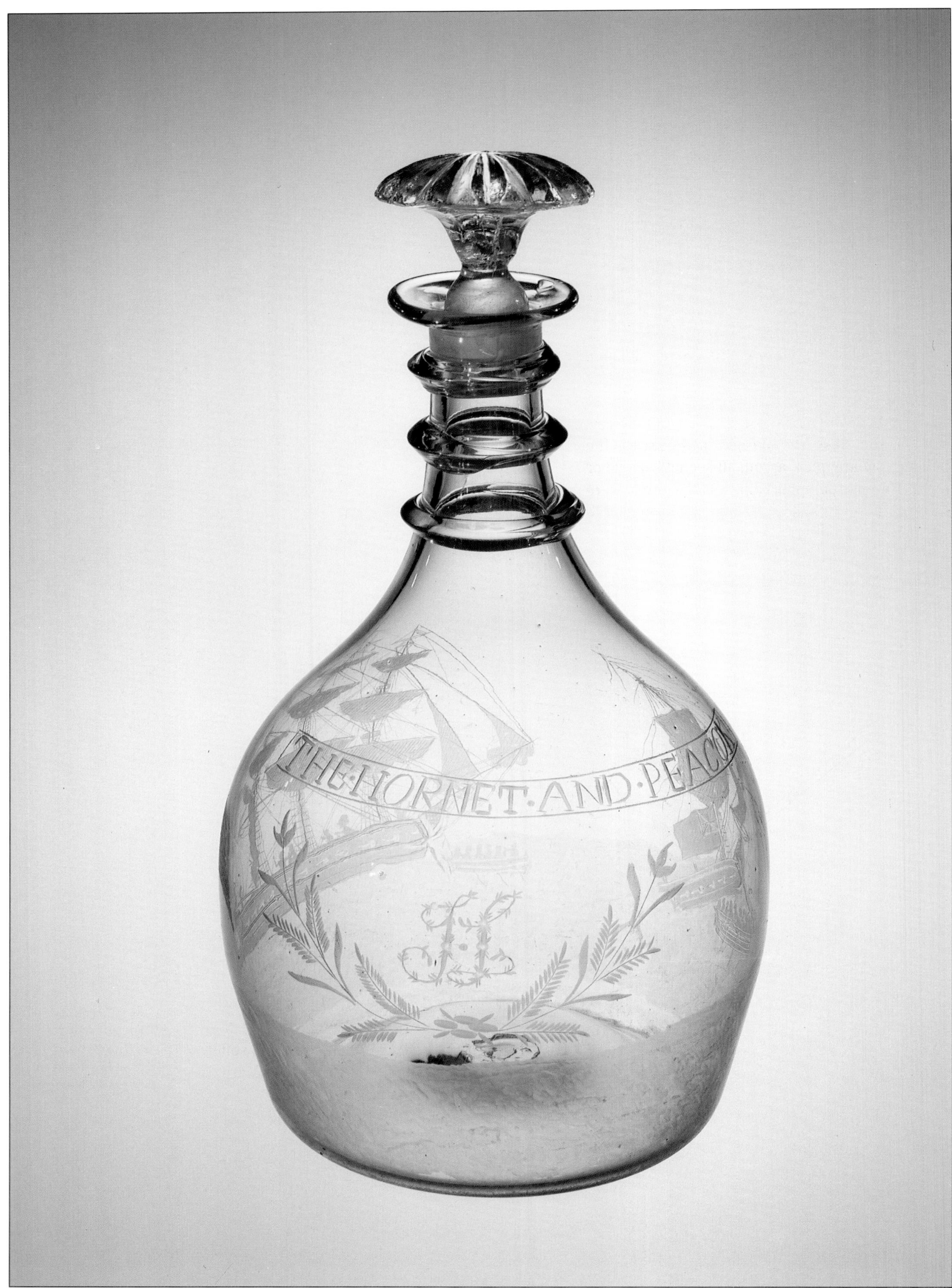
THE·HORNET·AND·PEACO

tor's Editions' offered at high prices by major alcoholic drink companies.

The least easy to date accurately and, because of their lack of asssociation, of least interest to collectors, are the purely pictorial flasks. However, the naïve charm of the motifs – ranging from cornucopias and baskets of fruit and flowers to birds, trees and animals, sometimes accompanied by a motto or title – still make them desirable.

A development from these designs was the production of bottles and flasks with a definite, if sometimes hidden, association: that of the Masonic Brotherhood. Many of the great republicans and statesmen who had founded the country and guided it in its infancy were Masons; by 1815 the society still retained its reputation for liberal thought, although the fashion for these emblematic wares subsided with the strength of the movement. By 1835 they were no longer being turned out. On one side of the flask the design incorporated the builder's square, pick, apron, all-seeing triangle or other Masonic paraphernalia; on the other were usually more broadly patriotic symbols – the American eagle was a favorite, as well as the American flag and the figure of Columbia, Patroness of Freedom.

But the largest and most varied selection of items is gathered together under the headings of 'commemorative' or 'historical' flasks. They included portraits of American heroes or soldier-statesmen: George Washington, 'Father of His Country'; Andrew Jackson, 'Old Hickory'; politician-statesmen such as Benjamin Franklin, John Adams, Henry Clay and Daniel Webster, and venerated foreigners like the French general Marquis de Lafayette, the Polish patriot Thaddeus Kosciuszko and the Hungarian politician Lajos Kossuth. A personality like Jenny Lind, 'the Swedish Nightingale,' earned the public's adoration and her own commemorative flask when she made her much heralded tour of the United States in 1850. Other historical flasks immortalized campaign slogans or economic ideologies, such as 'Under My Wings All Things Prosper' beneath a spread American eagle.

ABOVE: *Taylor/Ringgold flask, made c 1846–47 and attributed to Baltimore Glass Works. Major Samuel Ringgold was a popular hero. (Corning Museum of Glass.)*

LEFT: *Jenny Lind calabash bottle, c 1850–1 from the Isabella Glass Works or Pendleton Glass Works. Transparent aquamarine glass, mold-blown. (Corning Museum of Glass.)*

FACING PAGE: *Although commemorating a famous naval battle of the War of 1812, this decanter and stopper from the Birmingham Glass Works is in fact engraved and free-blown. (Corning Museum of Glass.)*

introduced, consumption had increased 10 times over. Jarves made that observation in 1852, in what was still the infancy of machine-pressed glass. By the turn of the century, sales had increased *100* times over, giving employment to thousands in the new factories that opened to cater to demand, in turn moving the center of the glass industry from the East Coast to the Midwest, meanwhile inspiring the invention of several other important technical processes with ramifications above and beyond that single industry. In short, the American preoccupation with producing goods that everyone could afford – in the cause of good business, of course, not charitable intentions – resulted in one of the single greatest contributions to the history of glassmaking and an important milestone in the development of the American hinterland.

No one knows exactly who invented the machine pressing of glass, but the date is somewhere between 1820 and 1825. According to later records, the first patent known to have been granted was to John Bakewell of the Pittsburgh Flint Glass Manufacturing Company, who patented an 'improved' method

ABOVE: *Mold-blown Bryan/ Sewell flask, c 1896. Souvenir of the 1896 Democratic presidential campaign. (Corning Museum of Glass.)*

RIGHT: *'Flora Temple' flask, 1859. Attributed to Whitney Glass Works; mold-blown. Commemorating Flora Temple, a record-breaking bay mare trotter. (Corning Museum of Glass.)*

FACING PAGE, ABOVE: *Railroad/ Lowell flask, c 1829–32; attributed to Connecticut Glass Works. Olive-amber glass, mold-blown. Commemorating the construction of the Boston to Lowell railroad. (Corning Museum of Glass.)*

FACING PAGE, BELOW: *A variety of Sandwich glass; date unknown. (Hirschl and Adler Galleries.)*

After 1850, the style began to change and the fad for portraits was replaced by ones for scenic motifs such as Pike's Peak and commemorating events like the Baltimore Fire or the Battle of Gettysburg.

The half-pint and pint colored bottles and flasks were made in two- and three-piece molds all over the East and Midwest; most commonly they appeared in brilliant shades of blue, green and purple. Some examples were even signed; the factories considered to have produced the best work include the Dyottville Glass Works near Philadelphia and the Lockport (New York) glassworks. Today these collectible whiskey containers have achieved the status of folk art.

GLASS: MACHINE-PRESSED GLASS

The importance of the mechanial pressing process to the American glassmaking industry can best be demonstrated by detailing a sample of the variety of wares produced, as well as recalling the words of Deming Jarves (founder of the highly successful Boston and Sandwich Glass Works), who said that in the years since the low cost product had been

for pressing furniture knobs. But since all physical evidence of the early patents was destroyed in the Washington Patent Office Fire of 1836, there may have existed earlier patents to improve upon. In any case, thereafter the process improved by leaps and bounds, and by 1828 cream jugs could be pressed with handles and bodies all in one piece. It was a busy year; at about the same time the first items of lacy glass were being experimented with – the 'pre-lacy' patterns, as they are known to collectors. In about 1830 to 1833, the first true lacy patterns appeared – the earliest family of items designed specifically to bring out the best in the mechanically molded glass instead of relying on the predictable and lackluster aping of cut glass, as had been the usual practice with cheaper substitutes up until then.

Lacy glass was given its particular personality and attraction by means of the stippled pattern of tiny raised dots on the underside or inner surface of the piece. Against this background an infinite choice of overpatterns could be imposed. The upper or exposed surface of the piece was smooth, but through it showed the brilliance of thousands of tiny diamonds. The early makers of this glass, which continued in popularity through the 1850s, included the New England Glass Company, the Boston and Sandwich Glass Company, the Pittsburgh Flint Glass Manufacturing Company and soon some smaller companies in the Midwest. The myriad overpatterns included flowers and leaves, geometric combinations – among them the extremely popular

ABOVE: *Three vases of machine-pressed glass. (Hirschl and Adler Galleries.)*

FACING PAGE, ABOVE: *early in the 20th century, in an attempt to emulate the success of Tiffany's favrile glass, companies producing cheap machine-pressed glass turned out huge numbers of 'taffeta' or 'carnival' glass.*

ABOVE RIGHT: *An opalescent and clear pressed butter dish of the type known as Holly Amber, but marketed as Golden Agate by the Inidana Tumbler and Goblet Company, Greentown, who made it. (Corning Museum of Glass.)*

FACING PAGE, BELOW: *The nesting hen was a popular pattern in both milk glass and the later carnival glass. Metallic purple (seen here) and a burnished marigold were two of the most popular iridescent shades.*

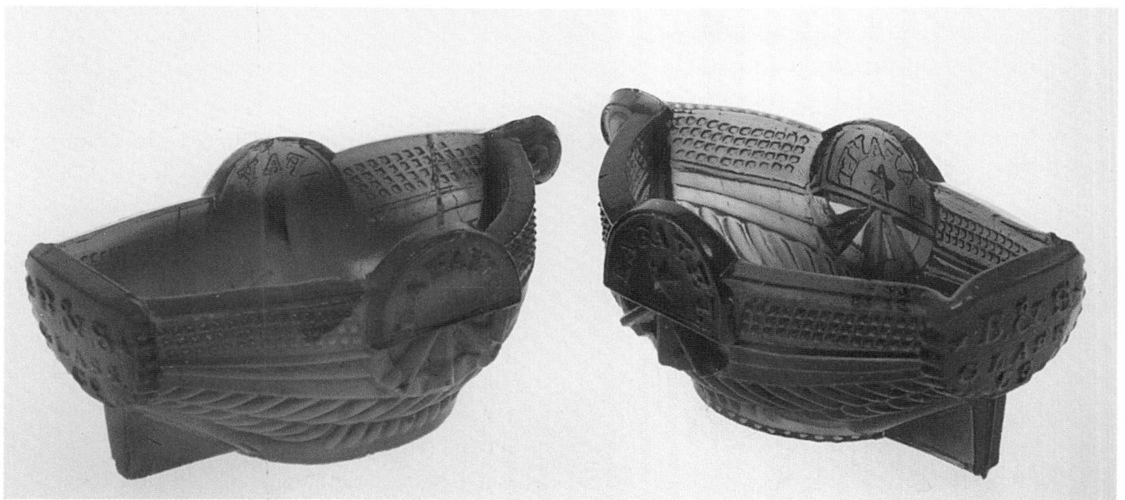

ABOVE RIGHT: *Makers of 'taffeta' or 'carnival' glass included the Imperial Glass Company, Fenton, Westmoreland, Northwood and Dugan.*

RIGHT: *Pair of 'Lafayet' boat salts made by the Boston and Sandwich Glass Company* c *1827–40 – the only pieces of pressed glass marked in the mold with the factory's name. (Sandwich Historical Society/ Glass Museum.)*

ABOVE: *An Amberina bottle made at the New England Glass Co., c 1885, and a Rubina Verde bottle and opalescent hobnail vase, both made by Hobbs, Brockumer and Co. c 1885. (The Bridgeman Art Library.)*

'peacock's eye' and 'horn of plenty' – American heroes' portraits and patterns based on contemporary porcelain. The lacy glass technique remained uniquely American for the space of about 10 to 15 years, and then spread across the ocean to England and the Continent.

Meanwhile, pressed glass production entered a new phase. The making of lacy glass was not as cost-effective as it might be, and public taste was moving toward heavier articles, in glass as in everything else. Taking cut glass as its inspiration but not following it slavishly, the machine-made version conquered in its new form. It was available colorless and in a rainbow of colors (greens, yellows, turquoise, blues and amethyst), transparent, marbled and opaque. The major introduction in terms of new pieces was the drinking glass; these had never been made in lacy glass. Whole 'table sets' were made – pitchers and decanters, water, champagne, wine and cordial glasses – as well as 'bar glasses,' beer and shot glasses among them. Celery vases, butter dishes, sugar bowls, punch bowls and compotes were other innovations. Pressed-glass window panes, usually with floral designs, were less common. Toward the end of the century animals – often ducks and chickens – made charming additions to the breakfast table in the form of covered butter dishes.

The turn of the century saw the first pieces in iridescent blue, amethyst and orange, later to become known as carnival glass, since some of the cheaper versions were often fairground prizes. Its heyday was from 1905 to the mid-1920s. Milk glass, the opaque white style of pressed glass, had actually been introduced around 1860, but it did not gain in popularity until the early 20th century.

Full automation came in 1915 with the invention of a machine to feed the melted glass direct from the tank to the pressing machine. From then on, most machine-pressed glass loses its collector's interest: common insulators, streetlight covers, cooking ware and milk bottles are today all made by this method (but who knows, in 50 to 60 years they, too, might be collectible!).

GLASS: ART GLASS

American art glass has a style and character all its own. While it was being made concurrently with British and Continental efforts, it is a rare occurrence for two pieces from opposite sides of the Atlantic to be confused. Once seen, the American product – although protean in the many shapes and shades it took and the techniques it utilized – is unmistakable and utterly distinctive. The English imitations it inspired – sometimes produced under license, sometimes not – are almost always distinguished by a different finish or perhaps a slightly different coloring: in the end, simply, by a notably different *feel*.

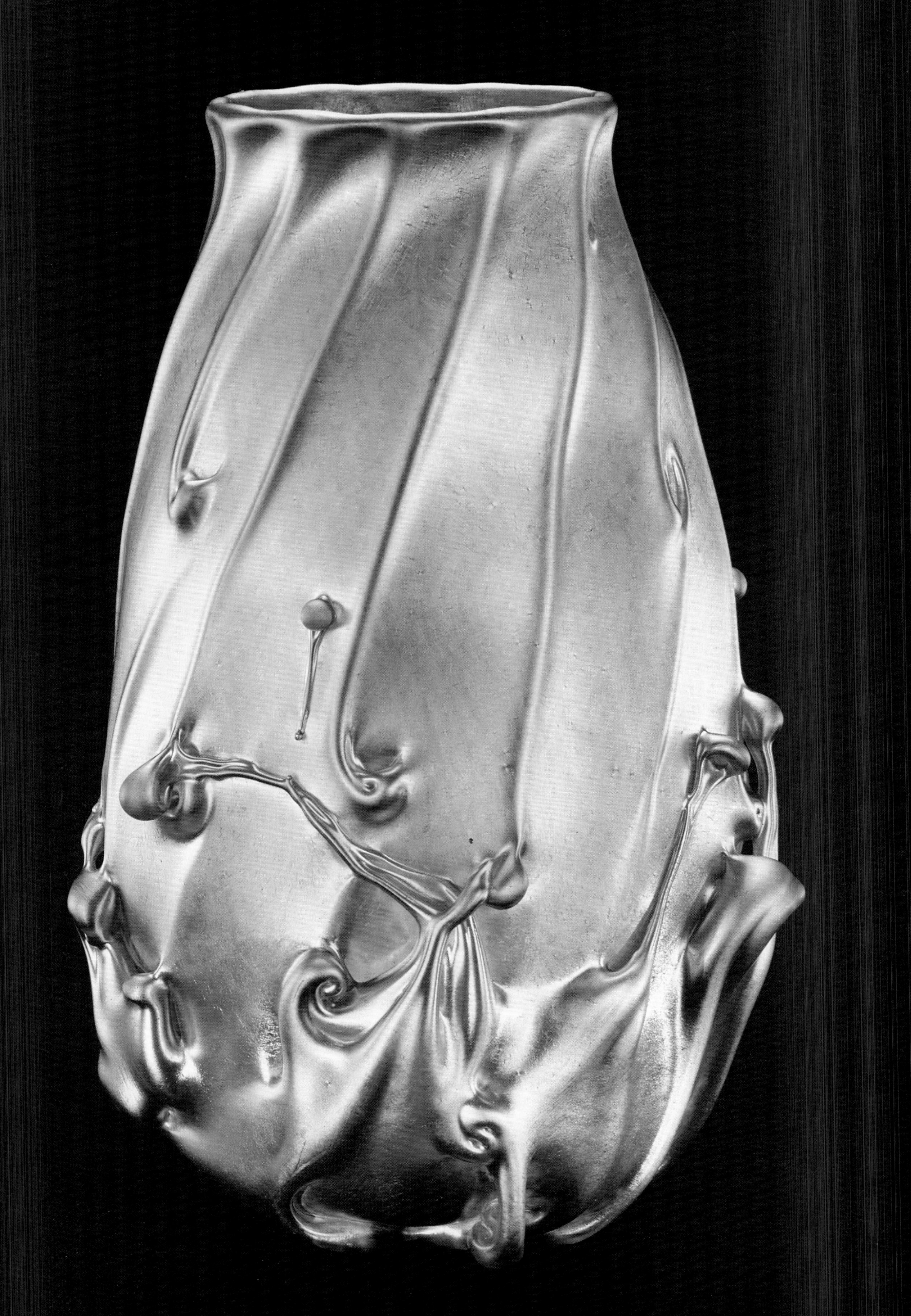

Although Louis Comfort Tiffany is, without a doubt, the first name that comes to mind when American art glass is mentioned, in fact the pieces that bear the Tiffany mark are not the first examples of the genre, nor do they necessarily command the highest prices. Several other designers and companies were there before him.

The history of American art glass is a complex and confusing one. It is a history of mergers, divisions and takeovers; of the head-hunting of some designers and the opening of new business ventures by others; of the cross-fertilization of ideas and of outright patent infringement. The following brief outline can only cover the major names and dates.

In the 55 or so years in which art glass was produced, there were five large companies involved and several smaller ones. The big names are, in some cases, big names still: the Mount Washington Glassworks (formed in 1837 by Deming Jarves of the Boston and Sandwich Glass Works); the Union Glass Company (founded 1826); Libbey Glass (registered in 1888, after changing its name from the New England Glass Company, founded 1818 as makers of molded, cut and machine-pressed glass; the Steuben Glass Company (founded 1903 and now part of Corning Glass Ltd.), and Tiffany Glass and Decorating Company (established in 1892 by Louis Comfort Tiffany, son of the prominent New York jeweler Charles L. Tiffany). Of the smaller glassworks, Quezal Art Glass (1901–25), Vineland Flint Glass Works (1897; art glass initiated 1924; company renamed Kimble Glass, 1931) and the A. Douglas Nash Co. (1928–32) are among those particularly prized by collectors.

Since many styles were produced by several companies, and it is usually the *type* of glass that actually determines the makers in which a collector specializes, it is probably of more interest and use to concentrate on the most popular styles produced in the years from 1883 to the mid-1930s.

Although there were prototypes and experiments beforehand, 1883 is the marker year as the birthdate of art glass. In that year Joseph Locke, a designer at the New England Glass Company, obtained a patent for a glass called 'Amberina', christened by the owner of the company, Edward Drummond Libbey. It realized immediate success when the entire stock was bought by Tiffany & Company, the New York jewelry store. After 1888, when the company was transferred to Toledo and its name changed, Amberina was marked with the name 'Libbey'. The vases, bowls and other objects – richly colored yellow or amber shading to red, or vice versa for 'Reverse Amberina' – were achieved by a clever appplication of reheating. It was not long before Mount Washington duplicated the process and produced its own version (later renamed

FACING PAGE: *Steuben vase, c 1910, made by Frederick Carder. Gold Aurene with tooled decoration and swirled ribbing. (Corning Museum of Glass.)*

LEFT: *Cologne bottle from the 1920s, by Steuben Glass. Colorless cut lead glass. (Corning Museum of Glass.)*

'Rose Amberina' after a civil case was brought against them by Libbey), and other factories began making their own variations. By the time the style had reached the end of its popularity, in around 1920, over 40 different types of glassware had been marketed in the distinctive Amberina colors.

Two years later Mount Washington scored a dual success with the appearance of its Peachblow and Burmese glass. While the former is characterized by translucent white glass shading to a rich pink, Burmese is a variation on the same theme, with yellow shading to a lighter salmon pink. Immediately the popular appreciation of the Mount Washington coup inspired imitations, with the copycat companies always managing to vary their products in depth of color and shading. A present was made to Queen Victoria of some Burmese ware, resulting in a license being granted to Thomas Webb and Company to produce their own version in Great Britain. In all their permutations and variations, these two styles account for a large part of collectible art glass.

ABOVE: *'Kew Blas' sherbet from the late 19th or early 20th century. Made by Union Glass Works. (Corning Museum of Glass.)*

FACING PAGE: *Tiffany peacock Favrile vase, made 1892–96. (Metropolitan Museum of Art, New York.)*

ABOVE: *Pair of overlay lamps from Sandwich Glass Company; opaque white cut to cranberry. On double marble base with gilt brass fittings. (Hirschl and Adler Galleries.)*

FACING PAGE: *Quezel Decorating Company blown goblet, c 1915–18. (Corning Museum of Glass.)*

FACING PAGE, LEFT: *Tiffany hanging lamp, of leaded glass; made in New York 1899. (Metropolitan Museum of Art, New York.)*

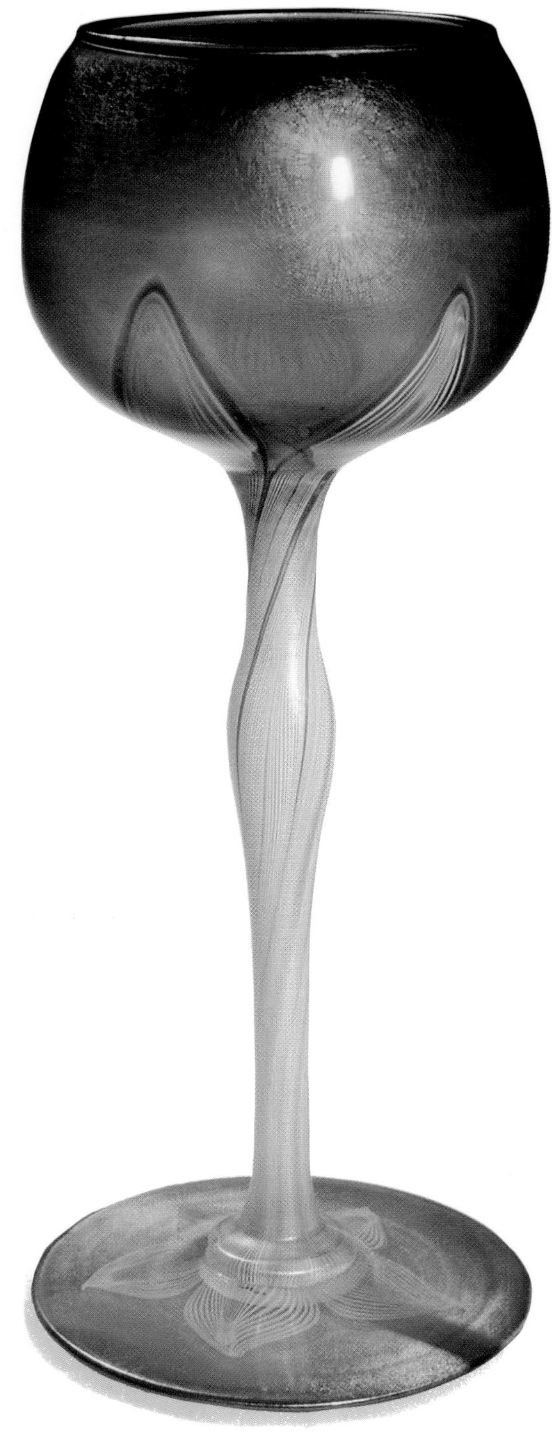

FACING PAGE: *Royal Flemish vase, c 1889–95 by the Mount Washington Glass Company. Blown, enameled lead glass with raised gilding. (Corning Museum of Glass.)*

RIGHT: *Four different types of late 19th-century colored glass: (left to right) peachblow bowl from Mount Washington Glass Works; Wild Rose peachblow vase from New England Glass Company; coral cruet by Hobbs, Brockunier and Company; Amberina vase from New England Glass Company. (Bridgeman Art Library.)*

BELOW: *Peacock leaded-glass window made by Louis Comfort Tiffany 1890–1900.*

The march was stolen on Tiffany's famous iridescent glassware by the registration in 1893 of Union Glass Company's Kew Blas ware (its name is an anagram of factory manager W. S. Blake), although the Tiffany Glass and Decorating Company had actually been making a few pieces of its Favrile glass since 1892. Louis Comfort took up the challenge by registering his glass in 1894 and, by means of superior marketing and a name recognized for quality as well as fine craftsmanship, soon overtook sales of Kew Blas glass. Today, both are highly regarded by experts, although the intimidation posed by Tiffany's success often caused the Union Glass Company styles to be somewhat derivative.

While the best of the Kew Blas glass features swirling, undulating leaf- and feather-like patterns in shades of green, tan, brown and blue, Tiffany's Favrile glass looked to far wider horizons, with a large number of patterns that differed greatly. Vases tended to be the main medium to display the jewel-like colors and nacreous finish of the glass; forms ranged from 'goosenecked' to ginger-jar-shaped, from wide-bodied and pinched-necked to fluted and footed. The decoration – sometimes applied, sometimes embedded – took the form of trailing lily pads or leaves, Middle-Eastern arabesques, peacock's feathers, golden scales, loops and/or threads. The colors varied from strong reds, yellows and blues to cloudier variations with golden overtones. Authentic examples from the Tiffany glassworks are signed with Tiffany's name or initials.

ABOVE: *Steuben vase, 1920s. (Corning Museum of Glass.)*

FACING PAGE: *Favrile vases and bowl by Louis Comfort Tiffany. (Metropolitan Museum of Art, New York.)*

By the turn of the century, the market for art glass was well established and several new makers joined the ranks, including the Imperial Glass Company (1901) of Bellaire, Ohio, with its freehand luster, Imperial Jewel, Egyptian and Moorish crackle vases; Fostoria Glass (1901) of Fostoria, Ohio; H.C. Fry Glass Company (1901) of Rochester, Pennsylvania, and Steuben Glass (1903), which was to survive as today's leading producer of ornamental glass. Its co-owner and leading designer, Frederick Carder (1864–1963), quickly introduced his Aurene glass to popular acclaim; blue and gold were the two characteristic colors overcast with a fine metallic sheen and sometimes applied decorative trailing. Carder remained with the company through its change of ownership (it was bought by Corning Glass in 1918) and until his retirement in 1933. He was responsible for an incredible wealth of types and styles of glassware, a few of which included Verre de Soie (*c*1916), Tyrian (*c*1917), Quartz (*c*1920), Cintra (*c*1917), Cluthra (*c*1930), Intarsia (*c*1930) and Grotesque (*c*1930s). He stands as one of the most technically and artistically gifted glassmakers of the modern age.

C H A P T E R S I X

CERAMICS

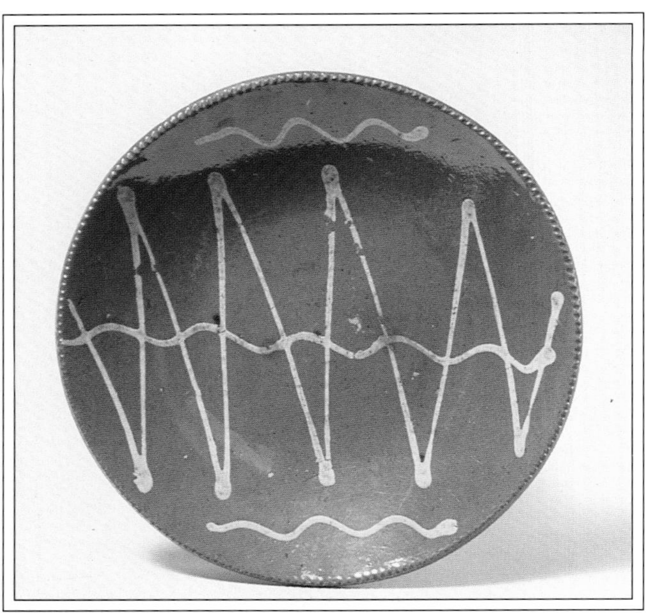

From the early days of settlement, a flourishing core of local potters established an American tradition in the face of competing foreign imports.

ABOVE: *Pennsylvania slipware plate from the late 18th century; artist unknown. (Everson Museum of Art.)*

FOLK POTTERY AND STONEWARE

In some sections of this book, it has been noted that some crafts – notably clock- and glassmaking – had belated starts due to the wealth of goods imported from England. The situation vis-à-vis ceramics is not as clean-cut. While it is true that commercial-style potteries, geared to mass-production and -distribution, were not really established until about 1830, largely because of the popularity and availability of Anglo-American wares, a flourishing core of local potters was established throughout the colonies from the earliest days of settlement. Their work is commemorated in placenames such as Potter's Creek, Pottertown, Jugtown, Clay City and – in four states! – Kaolin. Bricks were being made in Jamestown within two years of landing, while several tilemakers were in business there by 1649. Three potters were recorded as arriving in New England in 1635: Philip Drinker in Charlestown, Massachusetts, and William Vincent (or Vinson) and John Pride in Salem. By 1800, 250 potters were registered in the New England states alone. The manpower and the knowledge were certainly there.

As for the materials, these were also richly available. Red-burning clays for bricks, tiles and redware were everywhere under the widespread shale surface. The finer buff-burning clays reached from Vermont to Baltimore and west to Ohio, while true kaolin was discovered in 1738, in a vein that stretched from Virginia to Georgia. Regular transport between settlements was one of the first achievements of the colonial administration, so there was no trouble in moving raw materials from their source to where they were needed.

But the lack of a concentrated market – there were few large towns – and a preference for English goods among those who could afford them, meant that the combination of capability and clays did not result in the automatic growth of a native industry. Rather it meant the proliferation of many small craftsmen, producing and selling their wares within a circumscribed region. The major production area for these folk wares was New England, in particular Massachusetts and New Hampshire. The earliest type was the ubiquitous and utilitarian redware. Its color was caused by iron oxide, an impurity in the clay that came about when it was fired. Other less frequently encountered colors included green (copper oxide) and brown/yellow (manganese). Earthenware objects were simple and functional: kitchen and dairy items – flasks, bottles and storage jars – as well as tableware. Decoration was minimal, at first only finger-pinching or incising, and sometimes a thin interior glaze. Later, in the early 18th century, ornament became

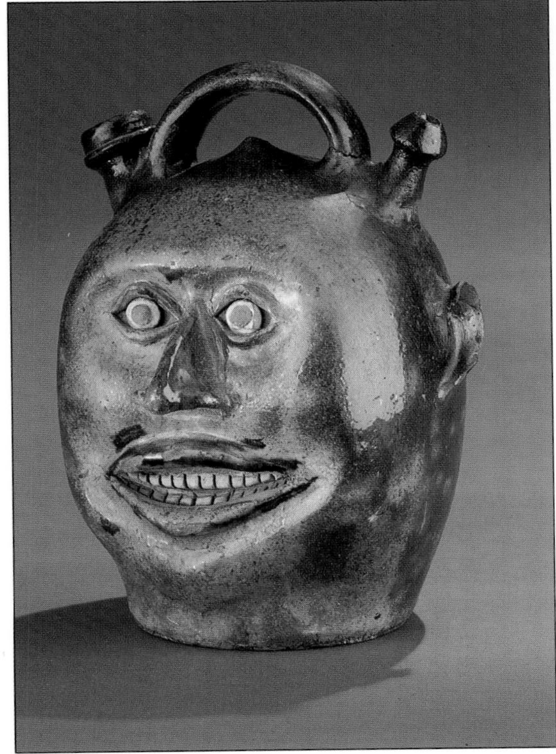

ABOVE: *Glazed redware coffee pot, c 1825. (Metropolitan Museum of Art, New York.)*

LEFT: *Face harvest jug, c 1850–75. Unidentified maker, probably South Carolina. The form of this jug appears to derive from the 'monkey jar', a plain earthenware vessel made to hold water, used in the West Indies and in the American South. (Abbey Rockefeller Museum.)*

ABOVE: *Sgraffito plate with floral design; Pennsylvania, 1818. (American Museum in Britain.)*

BELOW: *L. Smith tea canister, dated 1769, from Wrightstown, Bucks County, Pennsylvania (Henry Francis du Pont Winterthur Museum.)*

FACING PAGE: *Earthenware sgraffito plate, Pennsylvania* c *1800–25. (Henry Francis du Pont Winterthur Museum.)*

more ambitious, using several types of glazes based on metallic oxides or compounds of red lead, galeria and clay. Also introduced was *sgraffito*, in which a design was scratched through the outer glaze to expose the clay beneath.

Sgraffito ware was a particular specialty of the Pennsylvania Dutch potters, especially those of Bucks and Montgomery counties, where, from the late 18th century through the 1830s, they produced highly regarded examples. Plates and dishes were the main items decorated, usually produced for family celebrations like births and weddings. Slipware bird whistles, together with jugs, dishes and pie plates painted with hunting scenes, birds and animals, were other typical items. Moravian and Pietist sects produced their individualistic pieces in nearby regions.

Further south, in the Shenandoah Valley, the nine members of the Bell Family, comprising three generations, produced wonderful, highly glazed bowls, figures, jugs and dishes in celadon, green and deep orange glazes. Active from the very early 19th century through 1899, their work is much valued by collectors.

Stoneware was harder and finer than earthenware, fired at a temperature several times hotter. It was the focus of much experiment when it was feared that the lead glazing of earthenware might be poisonous. The first known dated piece of American stoneware was made by Joseph Thiekson of New Jersey in 1722, although it was probably in production during the first years of the century. Duller in color than earthenware – ranging from gray-white to buff to brown – it was eventually given a rough salt glaze.

The main stoneware centers were established near clay deposits in New York, Philadelphia and New Jersey, and later in Ohio. The finest examples were near-competitors to porcelain, although most stoneware was of a lower grade, used to make jugs, crocks, churns, whistles and banks. Perhaps the most important producers of the 'best' ware were the Crolyas – later Crolius – pottery. From 1730 to 1870, 15 members of the family carried on the tradition in a confusion of name and factory changes, nevertheless managing to remain throughout notable exponents of stoneware techniques.

The most usual decorations for stoneware were birds, animals, flowers, initials and dates, executed in a clear cobalt blue, or less frequently, brown. After 1850, the free-hand style changed to the cheaper stenciling. While the tradition of the small or individual potter was one that has continued to the present day in the United States, its all-pervasive character was mitigated by the wider availability of the products from commercial potteries.

LEFT: *Jug, 1850–59, stoneware with salt glaze and slip decoration. (Bennington Museum.)*

RIGHT: *Pot with salt glaze and slip decoration, made c 1850–59. (Bennington Museum.)*

BELOW RIGHT: *Creamware plate made in Liverpool, UK, for the US market – note the US flag. Made c 1800. (American Museum in Britain.)*

CERAMICS: COMMERCIAL POTTERY AND STONEWARE

The beginnings of a truly commercial attitude to the production of tableware could be credited to the development of creamware manufacture in the United States, following its overwhelming success in England. By 1771, John Bartlam, one of Josiah Wedgwood's 'insolvent master potters', was reproducing the formula of his erstwhile employer in Charleston, South Carolina. The pirate creamware firm had a short and rocky history, but engendered enough enthusiasm for the product to beget several other creamware factories in Philadelphia and New York before the end of the 18th century. By the third decade of the 19th century production had spread to other states, but its popularity diminished with the upsurge in other wares.

Spurred on by the continued popular preference for foreign printed wares, the American potters of the first decades of the 19th century studied the market assiduously. Makers of earthenware and stoneware realized that if they could approach the quality and style of the Staffordshire potteries, which produced a huge variety of wares – from the early black-painted creamware to the outrageously popular 'Historical Blue', all with patterns tailor-made for American buyers – they would be granted a slice of a captive market. It was an uphill struggle, however, despite a series of punishing tariffs imposed between 1816 and 1824, more English wares were imported monthly in 1825 than annually in 1790.

In the 1830s and 1840s, David Henderson's American Pottery Company of Jersey City, New Jersey, produced transfer-printed blue-and-white wares similar to those of Staffordshire. They included plates with repeated floral designs as well as jugs and bowls with patriotic and historical subjects; the latter included eagles and shields or valedictories to great leaders, like General Lafayette or the recently deceased president William Henry Harrison. But try as they might, these attempts could only dent the tenacious hold of the English Midlands potteries on the American market. Independent they might be politically, but the Americans still looked to England before they set their table.

The case was quite different for the Rockingham-type wares turned out in Bennington, Vermont. The earliest kiln began operations there in 1793, under the direction of Captain John Norton. After preliminary production of earthenware, it had settled down by 1815 to the almost exclusive making of stoneware.

Bennington's real success began in 1843, when Christopher Webber Fenton and Julius Norton, the grandson of John, entered into partnership and engaged John Harrison from England's Copeland factory to supervise the day-to-day running of their pottery. It soon became known for its mottled flint enamel glaze on stoneware, and later for its Parian ware and Belleek-style porcelain. A patent for the first process was obtained in 1849, although some experimental pieces were certainly made prior to that date. The glaze was different from similar efforts by contemporary potteries in the strength and depth of its colors, shades of green, blue, yellow and orange that washed over the recumbent lions, deers and cows adorning its flasks, jugs and pitchers. In time, the term 'Bennington' was used to describe all American versions of this 'Rockingham'-style ware – produced in quantity in Ohio, Pittsburgh and Baltimore – until its fall from popularity in 1900.

CERAMICS: PORCELAIN

If the cheaper products of the American potteries had a difficult time asserting their worth against an influx of foreign imports, the situation of locally produced porcelain was made even more impossible. As in England, export ware from China was well regarded by those who could afford better things. Before the Revolution, imports were siphoned to the colonies via the ports of Great Britain, but soon after Independence, eager merchants were plying their own trade. The first American ship left for the East in 1784; by 1790, 28 ships had made the long voyage, returning laden with lacquer, tea, silks and cottons, and porcelain. Commemorative bowls and jugs, and entire services decorated with 'heraldic' arms, ships, eagles and imitations of European-style patterns were off-loaded in the ports of New York, Philadelphia, Boston, Charleston and Norfolk to grace the tables of the great and gracious, from the bourgeoisie of the North to the plantation society of the South. By the 1850s, literally tons of Chinese-made porcelain had made its way into American homes.

There was another, if somewhat lesser, threat in trade with European porcelain factories. Delicate and more expensive than the Chinese export ware, the products of Liverpool and Worcester in England and of Sèvres, Nast and Dagoty in France could only be afforded by the highest in the land – but that included American presidents. Services for Washington and his successors were ordered from the newly formed and sympathetic French Republic, although the sixth president, John Quincy Adams, sought to extend patronage further and ordered a table setting from Meissen. But whether from

ABOVE: *Porcelain sweetmeat dish, 1769–72. This bonbon dish is one of the group that has been attributed to Bonnin and Morris in Philadelphia. All reflect the style of English porcelain factories, although this porcelain is less delicate than the English examples. (Brooklyn Museum.)*

FACING PAGE, TOP: *Basket of soft paste porcelain by Bonnin & Morris, Philadelphia, c 1769–72. (Henry Francis du Pont Winterthur Museum.)*

FACING PAGE, BELOW: *Porcelain plate from China, 1800–15, emblazoned with the American eagle to appeal to the US market. (Henry Francis du Pont Winterthur Museum.)*

France, England or Germany, the effect was the same – there was little encouragement for funding a native industry.

The earliest American experiments in true hard-paste porcelain were the work of andrew Duché (1710–78), who, like his father Antoine, was a proficient stoneware potter. Supported by the founder of the colony of Georgia, he established a pottery in Savannah in 1738, located several veins and quarries of potting clays and quickly produced some pieces to show influential people on both sides of the Atlantic. Outside of a mere handful of survivals of his work in either medium, little more is known of him. Even less is known of the potter Samuel Bowen (who took over the works in 1743, after Duché had left for England), except that Bowen too appears to have sought approval abroad, since he was awarded a medal from the English Society for the Encouragement of Arts, Manufactures and Commerce for his work in china.

For a more documented account of porcelain-making, backed by contemporary records of names and dates, and a cache of some 20 surviving specimens, we must wait until 1770 and the establishment of the Southwark, Philadelphia, chinaworks

of Gouse Bonnin and George Anthony Morris. They employed nine master workmen and 'painters in blue or enamel', and acquired an agent, Archibald M'Elroy, to sell their wares in Philadelphia. From newspaper advertisements, it seems that their effort lasted a mere two years; today only blue-and-white examples of their work remain.

Despite the fragments of porcelain unearthed at the site of the Jersey Porcelain & Earthenware Company (1825–28), and newspaper accounts of its 'French-style' porcelains, the palm for the first successful china-making firm must go to the Philadelphia company of William Ellis Tucker (1800–32), who also specialized in wares that compared with the 'best specimens of French china'. He established partnerships with John Hulme (Tucker & Hulme, 1828–29) and with Alexander Hemphill (Tucker & Hemphill, 1831–38, which continued six years after Tucker's untimely death in 1832), producing tea services, vases and – most famously – pitchers. The majority of his pieces were decorated with floral patterns and made lavish use of gilding.

The Bennington pottery of Norton & Fenton (later Lyman & Fenton, and, from 1853 to 1858, the United States Pottery Co.), more renowned today for its stoneware and flint enamel decoration, was also an enthusiastic producer of Parian biscuit-style statuary from 1843, and of blue-and-white porcelain from 1853. By the last five years of the factory's life, it was also turning out highly decorated and gilded table services, all made with clays and materials mined in New England.

Among the welter of small companies that sprang up from the late 1840s to the 1860s, two must be singled out which opened up the sales of American porcelain considerably. By attempting to sell their wares on a wider commercial basis and less as acknowledged luxury, they gave the business a much-needed push, producing everything from door knobs to inkwells, from table services to figurines. They were Charles Cartlidge & Company (1848–56), whose articles were largely in 'biscuit' porcelain, and William Boch & Brother (1850–62), both of Greenpoint (today Brooklyn), New York. The latter firm was taken over by the Union Porcelain Works in 1862; its production of bone china was then changed to hard-paste, which it continued to produce until its closure in 1910.

After the Philadelphia Centennial Exhibition in 1876 – the source of so much innovative and derivative work in the American decorative arts – there was much popular fascination with Belleek porcelain from Ireland. Attempts to reproduce it were fairly successful, largely due to the fact that its American birth pangs were attended by the Irish potter William Bromley, who had developed the

ABOVE: *Blue and white pitcher, parian ware c 1850. (Metropolitan Museum of Art, New York.)*

LEFT: *Vase-shaped pitcher by Joseph Hemphill, c 1833, Philadelphia, PA. (Henry Francis du Pont Winterthur Museum.)*

FACING PAGE: *Vase-shaped pitcher by William Ellis Tucker, Philadelphia PA, c 1825–30. Painted and gilded porcelain. (Hirschl & Adler Galleries.)*

1876, when the movement taking place in England received much publicity. A few potters in the United States became as determined as their English and Continental fellows to cast off the restrictions of mass-production, and to gamble with shape and glaze.

The first kiln at Rookwood was fired on November 25, 1880. The firm was established by Maria Longworth Nichols (1849–1932), a prominent socialite and friend of the arts, and named after her family estate because 'it was reminiscent of Wedgwood'. As a business venture it was a poor investment – a rich woman's fancy, subsidized by her father – but as an influence on the decorative arts it became nationally important. It was taken seriously by the artistic establishment, winning the *Medale d'Or* at the Paris Exposition in 1900, and was celebrated as an inspiration by the architect-designers Charles and Henry Greene for their furniture. Mrs. Nichols

ABOVE: *Japanese peasant figure vase, 1889 by Rookwood Pottery; decorator Mathew A. Daly. (Everson Museum of Art.)*

original. He assisted the Trenton firm of Ott & Brewer in producing its first piece in 1882; by 1887 it was being made by Walter Lenox and in 1888 by Knowles, Taylor & Knowles, whose version, known as 'Lotus Ware', was probably the most delicate and original. The styles in which it was made in the 1890s ally it to contemporaneous products of the Art Pottery movement.

CERAMICS: ART POTTERY

The best-known company name in American art pottery is Rookwood. For a luminous decade, the undisputed capital of art pottery was Cincinnati, Ohio. There, in the years between 1879 and 1889, six art potteries, including Rookwood, were operating. The other five were the Avon Pottery, the Cincinnati Art Pottery, the Mary Louise McLaughlin's factory, the Matt Morgan Art Pottery and the T. J. Wheatley Pottery. It was a brief explosion of Arts and Crafts fervor, however. By 1890 all but Rookwood had closed.

The enthusiasm for 'Studio Ware' really began after the Centennial Exhibition in Philadelphia in

RIGHT: *A Rookwood vase exhibited at the Paris Exhibition 1900. (Hamlyn Publishing Group.)*

FACING: *Double-tiered 'cucumber green' vase from the Grueby Faience Company, Boston, 1897–1909. (Hirschl and Adler Galleries.)*

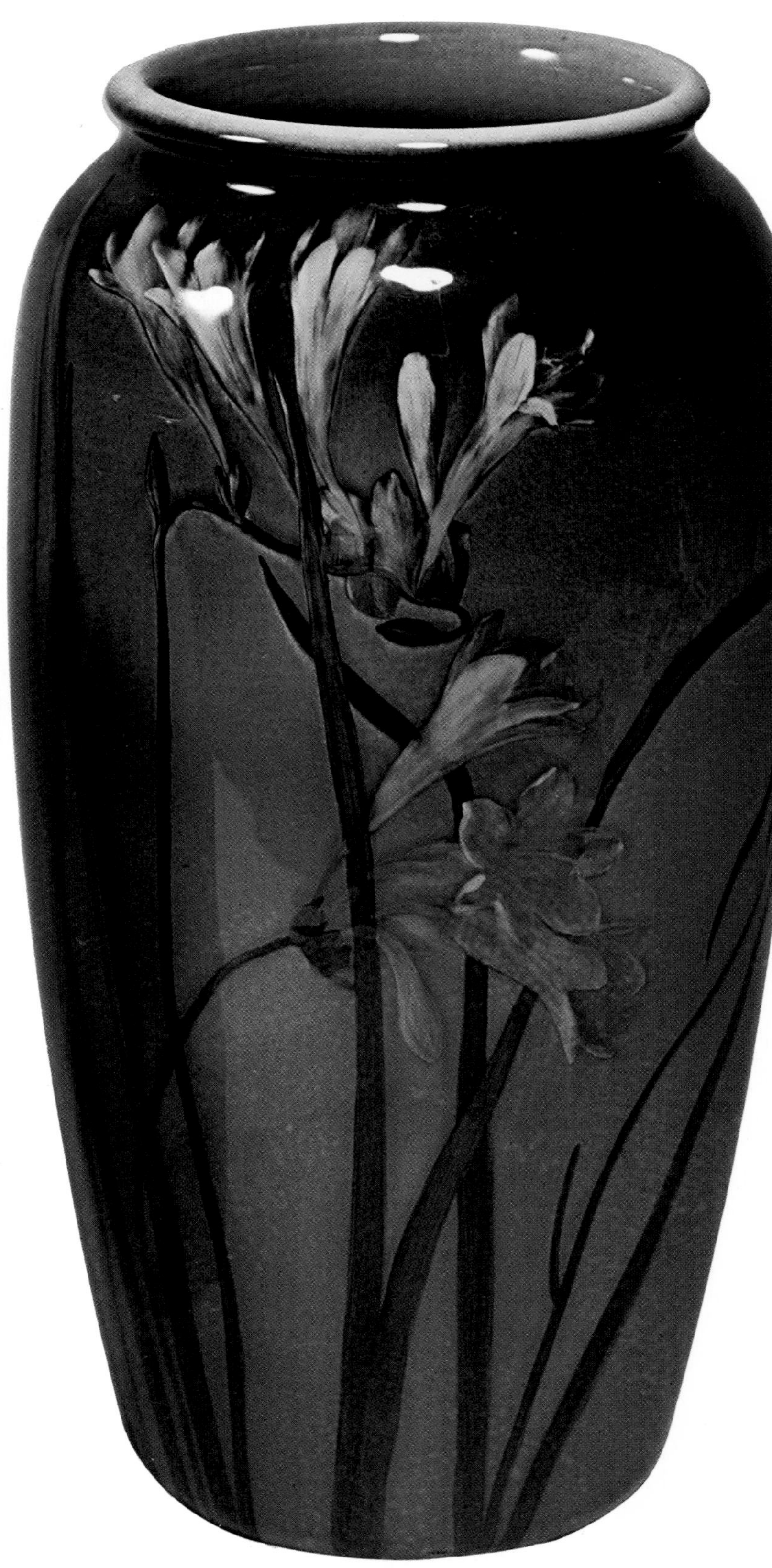

ABOVE: *Rookwood vase exhibited at the Paris Exhibition of 1900. (Hamlyn Publishing Group.)*

possessed a vision, if not business acumen, and her lack of attention to the almighty dollar gave the company an invaluable start. When it was sold to its general manager William Watts Taylor in 1889, finances dictated it be run more circumspectly. But by that time it had established its reputation as a high-quality maker of unique wares, each piece one-of-a-kind, signed and dated.

Rookwood products were primarily display wares – vases, bowls and plates. The styles varied from the early underglaze slipwares on dark grounds – pinkish-white Cameo and orange-brown Mahogany to the gold-speckled Adventurine of the late 1880s. Oriental shapes displayed floral motifs on backgrounds called Iris, Sea Green and Aerial Blue. Matte glazes were introduced in 1896 and transparent ones appeared from 1904. Among the most desirable signatures to appear on its pieces are those of the head decorator Albert R. Valentien, Laura A. Fry, Artus Van Briggle, Clara Chapman Newton and Kuitaro Shirayamadani. Although Taylor died in 1913, Rookwood's standard of production remained high until the early 1920s; after that it tapered off in originality and execution, until the factory closed in 1941.

The Rookwood look spread its influence through its workers. Van Briggle left to found his own pottery in Colorado Springs in 1901; Laura Fry joined William A. Long to found the Lonhuda Pottery at Steubenville, Ohio; in 1895 this merged with another factory at Zanesville, Ohio, and was renamed Louwelsa. Their decorations and glazes were very derivative of the Rookwood style, but an iridescent lusterware invented for the factory by the French designer Jacques Sicard (named 'Sicardo') was one of the happiest contributions of the American Art Pottery movement. Two more Zanesville companies produced art pottery: the J. B. Owens Pottery, whose Utopian ware (1896–1907) harks back to both Rookwood and Louwelsa, and the Roseville Art Pottery, whose Rozane and Rozane Royale (*c*1900) are the stars of an otherwise rather lackluster catalog.

In Massachusetts, the Chelsea Keramic Art Works, in Chelsea, devised several 'Oriental-style' glazes, among them a luscious *sang-de-boeuf* and a 'Japanese' crackleware. Renamed the Chelsea Pottery in 1891 and then Dedham Pottery (after moving to Dedham in 1895), it drifted more and more toward the production of commercial blue-and-white ware. Art Nouveau-style tiles were the preoccupation of both the John G. Low Factory of Chelsea, Massachusetts, and of Grueby Faience and Tile Company, of East Boston, Massachusetts (Grueby also produced lovely matté-glazed vases). Their swirled squares decorated many a fireplace in the years around the turn of the 20th century.

TOP LEFT:
Rookwood stoneware vase. (Everson Museum of Art.)

LEFT:
Futura vase from the Roseville Pottery Co., Ohio, c 1925–30. (Alastair Duncan/collection of John P. Axelrod.)

TOP RIGHT:
Rookwood vase with more ornate ornamentation than many. (Alastair Duncan.)

BELOW: *Late 19th-century Rockwood vase.*

C H A P T E R S E V E N

T E X T I L E S

Rugs born of thrift and samplers from a genteel heritage – and quilts to keep everyone warm.

ABOVE: *Linen sampler from Newport, Rhode Island, embroidered with silks; signed by Hannah Taylor, dated August 18, 1774. (The American Museum in Britain.)*

ABOVE: *Late 19th-century sampler. (Shelburne Museum.)*

SAMPLERS AND STITCHED PICTURES

As in so many other areas, the American colonies tried hard to ape the fashions and pursuits of the middle-class country life so many of them left behind. This extended to the genteel education of their daughters, who were expected to master the basic tenets of needlework before they were let loose on the three R's. At school they received further drilling in the finer points of embroidery and cross-stitching, learning to combine various techniques in a single article – the sampler – to display their skills and sense of composition.

Samplers from 17th-century England are rare, and those from the United States are even rarer. Among the earliest known is that executed by Loara Standish, the daughter of Captain Myles Standish, the Pilgrim father. Dated 1653, the sampler is typical of early examples up to and including the early 18th century. Consisting of a long, narrow linen panel, it existed merely to demonstrate the child's conquest of the alphabet and certain stitches; decoration for its own sake was minimal. The needlework was arranged in horizontal bands with an occasional flower spray in cross-stitch or a design in drawn-thread work to fill in a short line.

From 1750 to 1770 the youthful needlewoman was allowed more creative freedom. The linen or canvas cloth metamorphosed into a squarer, or at least oblong, shape. Birds, animals, human figures and buildings appeared more frequently, sometimes

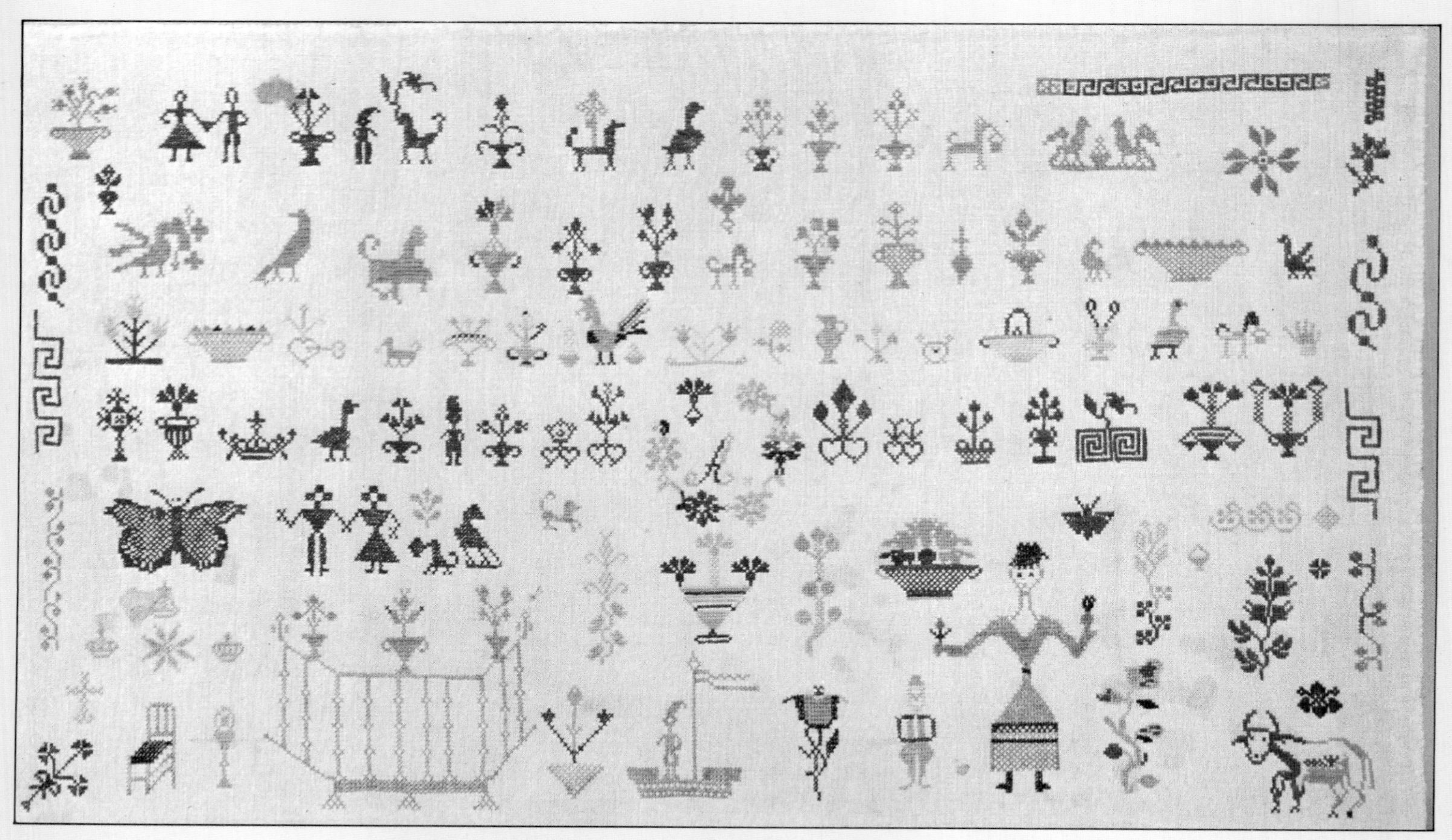

The Prince of peace is come
Ye nations shout and sing.
Let men and angels join their songs.
To hail this glorious King.

Now in the opning fpring of life
Let every flowret bloom
The budding virtues in thy breast
Shall yield the beft perfume
Charlotte Gubb
Wafhington City July 20th 1813

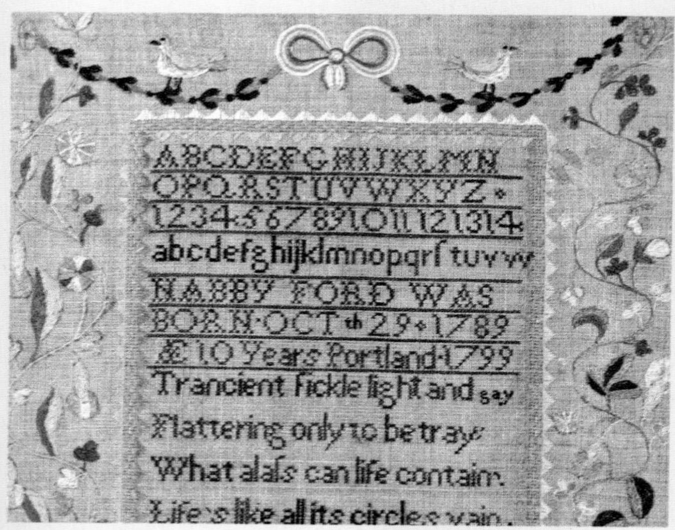
ABCDEFGHIJKLMN
OPQRSTUVWXYZ
1234567891011121314
abcdefghijklmnopqrſtuvw
NABBY FORD WAS
BORN OCT th 29 1789
Æ 10 Years Portland 1799
Trancient fickle light and gay
Flattering only to betray
What alafs can life contain
Life's like all its circles vain.

dominating the lettering and numbers. This, too, began to change; no longer was the alphabet the sole exponent of literacy. A motto, verse from scripture, the Ten Commandments or the Lord's Prayer – or, later, a selection from Isaac Watts's highly popular *Divine Songs for Children* – was also considered appropriate. The biblical and religious themes were extended into the pictorial realm by the inclusion of such stalwarts as Adam and Eve (either clothed or nude), Noah and the Ark, Tobias and the Angel and the Flight Into Egypt, as well as flower gardens (sometimes representing Eden) and hunting scenes.

Often as many as four or five different types of lettering appear on the same sampler: lower case, capitals, script, florid capitals and/or numerals, and finally a verse or motto bringing up the end with a fine flourish. In the late 18th and early 19th centuries, this extended series of letters often overtook the decorative element, so that the sampler became again a series of horizontal strips, now bordered by a bright, florid border of leaves and flowers.

By the 1840s and 1850s the pictorial element was again in the ascendant. Grecian temples, steepled churches, comfortable houses bordered by white fences and stately trees reflected the young needlewoman's ideals of the good life as much as her own circumstances. Verses and scenes worked together to extol the virtues of chastity, obedience, love and friendship. The mixture of saccharine sentiment and austere reflection was singularly youthful and entirely Victorian. After this time, however, the idiosyncracy of the sampler was supplanted by the repetitive ease of Berlin woolwork, and the days of these signed schoolgirl masterpieces were numbered.

Concurrent with the popularity of the sampler was the taste for pictorial panels or pictures. These were natural follow-ups for young women reared on the discipline of samplers. Finer, of course, than their youthful precursors, they made use of delicate floss or twisted silk and were worked in a catalog of stitches on canvas, silk, linen or satin. Sometimes the sky, sea or rolling pastures were filled in with paint, and occasionally jewelry, stars or flowers were picked out with beads or sequins. Among the most common of these are the 'mourning pictures' executed to commemorate the death of a loved one – either a private or a public loss. Many were dedicated to George Washington and, to a lesser extent, other heroes of the early republic. The fashion for these highly worked 'embroidered paintings' was a relatively short one, however, over even more quickly than the vogue for the childish sampler. By 1830 they too had succumbed to the ease of Berlin woolwork.

TEXTILES: QUILTS AND COVERLETS

Although the word quilt suggests a patchwork to most people, the terms are not mutually inclusive. Patchwork is a *type* of quilt, but quiltwork includes a far larger inventory than the bedcovers made from multicolored squares sewn together either in a pattern or a higgledy-piggledy manner. Other types include plain fabric couch-quilted or appliquéd, trapunto work, or one of several permutations or combinations of all five. By definition, a quilt is composed of two layers of material, with a filling of wool or some other wadding providing warmth and thickness. The technique has been known for hundreds of years and been practiced from China throughout Europe and Britain to reach – what many feel to be – its finest form in the examples of North America.

Two other types of coverlet were popular in the New World before the arrival of the quilt. They were the crewelwork bedspread, with matching hangings – probably the most prized form of counterpane throughout the 17th and most of the 18th centuries – and the wool-on-wool coverlet, with patterns worked in looped yarn onto a background of natural colored wool. The effect was that of a woven pile rug. Most of the latter were made in New England in the Connecticut River Valley, and date from 1724 to the early 19th century.

Toward the late 18th century the first prototypes of American-style quilts began to appear. The wool filling was covered in all-white or single-colored glazed cotton or linen. The stitching was extremely fine, covering the entire large square with a rich

FACING PAGE, TOP: *This cross-stitch sampler is not signed or dated, but is thought to be a 19th-century piece from Pennsylvania. (The American Museum of Britain.)*

FACING PAGE, CENTER LEFT: *19th-century sampler by Rebecca Van Reed Gresemer from Pennsylvania. Some sections are hand painted on the fabric. (The American Museum in Britain.)*

FACING PAGE, BELOW LEFT: *Alphabet sampler by 10-year-old Nabby Ford, completed in 1799. (The American Museum in Britain.)*

FACING PAGE, BELOW RIGHT: *Sampler by Charlotte Glubb, made 1813 using a variety of stitches. (The American Museum in Britain.)*

BELOW: *White Trapunto coverlet, probably from the late 19th century. (Thomas K. Woodard Antiques, New York.)*

ABOVE: *Appliquéd cotton quilted coverlet, c 1820–30. (Christie's, New York.)*

pattern of graceful floral arabesques and leaf patterns, sometimes interspersed or bordered by geometric patterns of squares or diamonds. Occasionally additional pieces of colored material were appliquéd onto the plain base, thus bringing out the plumage of birds and the petals and leaves of flowers. A more hardy variation of the plain-colored quilt was the type known as 'Linsey-woolseys', with dyed and glazed woollen fabric on one side and coarser fabric on the other, with carded wool in between. The stitching was accomplished in strong linen thread.

Copper-printed materials, with the pattern executed in a single color – blue, red or magenta – were simply quilted in square or chevron patterns, so that the design of the material was not disturbed by the stitching.

Chintz was a popular fabric in the 18th century, for dresses and sometimes home furnishings, although it was expensive and easily spoiled. While full chintz coverlets made their way onto some beds, the average housewife could only afford off-cuts. Thus was born the classic patchwork quilt. At first, the central motif was often a Rising Sun or Star of Bethlehem, appliquéd to the squares of the plain white material that formed the background.

Diamond-shaped pieces of chintz and/or calico formed the body of the star, while others were used to make a border. This was the style of patchwork associated with the early 19th century.

With experience and confidence, the patterns became more ambitious, and by the 1820s making quilts had begun to develop into a cottage craft with its own special techniques and skills, and by 1830 patterns for quilt blocks were published in *Godey's Lady's Book*. Household objects were often used as patterns and templates, and daughters were given the chores of cutting patterns and chalking designs. The squares that formed the main patterns were assembled into blocks, then arranged in strips together with sections of the white background, before they were quilted into the final design. The background quilting stitch was often very elaborate: names like the cross bar, diamond, diagonal and double and triple crossbars feature in specialist descriptions.

The arrangement of block sections were given names: among the best known are Feather Wreath, Feather Star, Wheel of Fortune, Pineapple, Star Crescent, Pine Tree (also called Tree of Life), Cactus Rose, Rose of Sharon, Log Cabin, Oak Leaf, Bellflower, Dove of Peace and Thrown Fan. These

ABOVE: *'Tree of life', an early 19th-century appliqué spread with stuffed work. (Thomas K. Woodard Antiques, New York.)*

LEFT: *North Carolina lily pattern quilt, c 1840. (The American Museum in Britain.)*

BELOW: *Robbing Peter design quilt from 1886. (The American Museum in Britain.)*

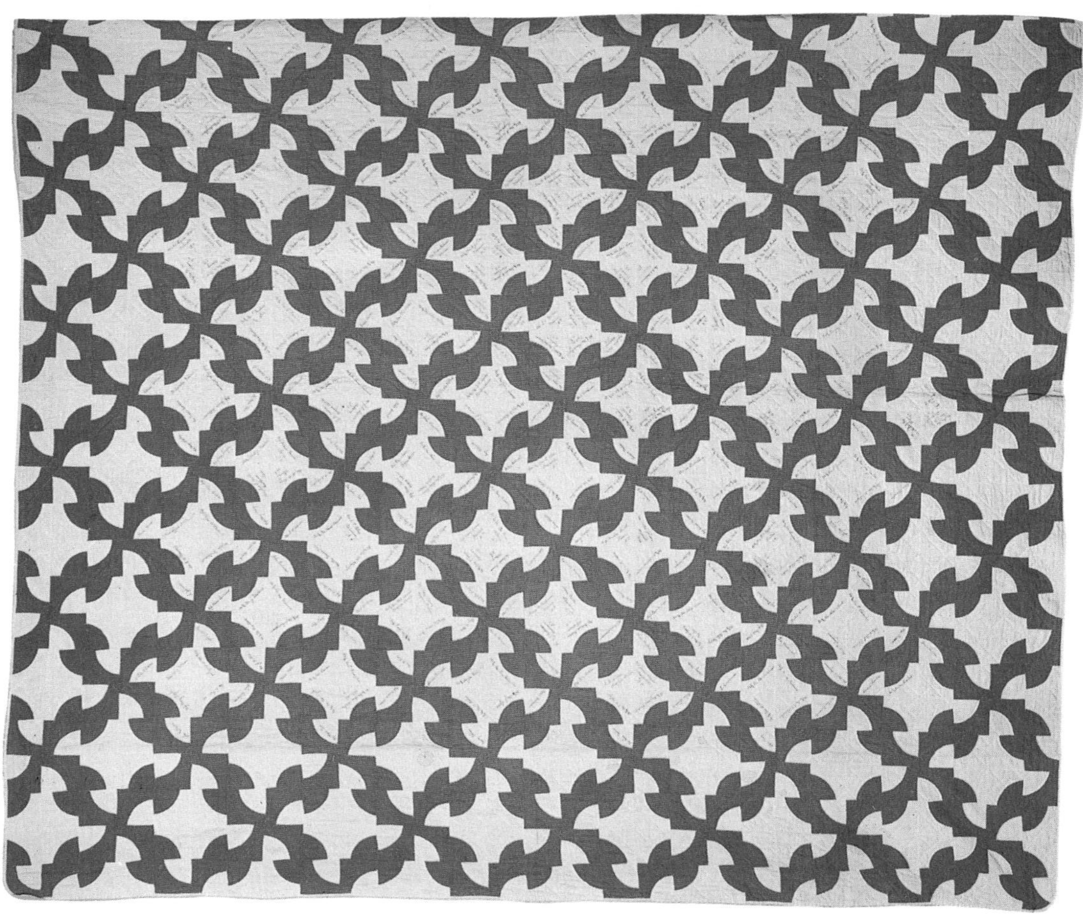

FACING: *Log cabin barn-raising design quilt from 1863. (The American Museum in Britain.)*

[p.140 (110)]

Top right: *A Baltimore Bride quilt, made in 1847. (The American Museum in Britain.)*

Below right: *Amish quilt with fan pattern, made in Ohio* c *1920. (American Folk Art.)*

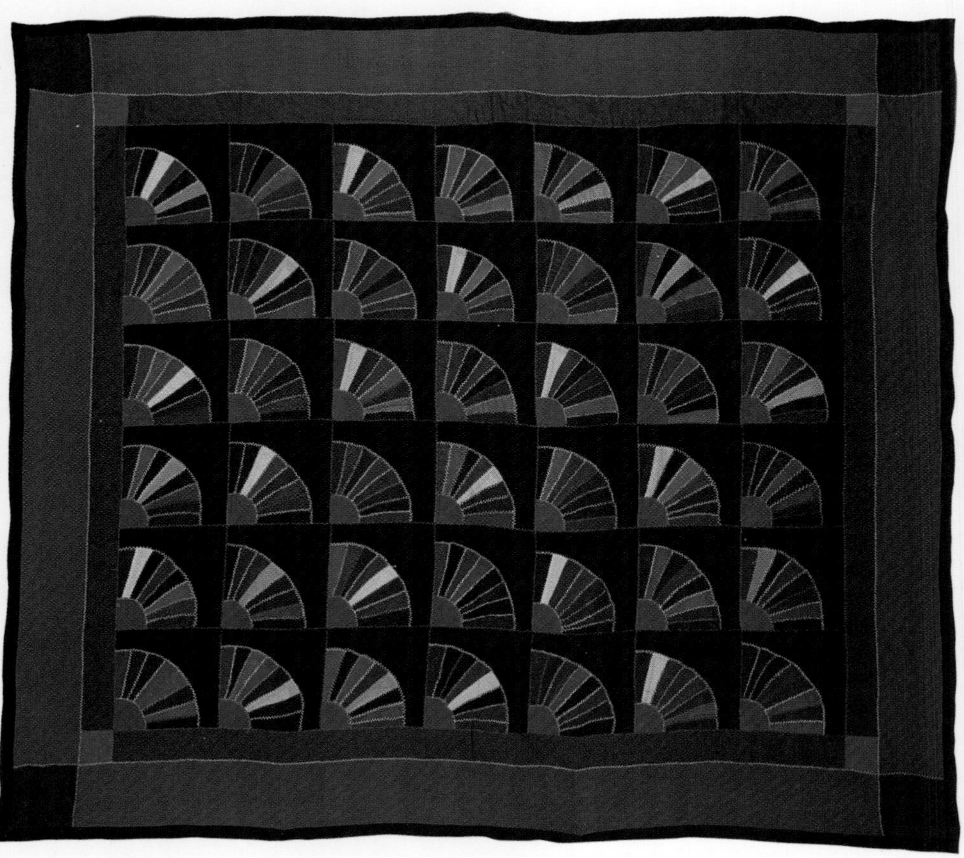

ABOVE RIGHT: *19th-century Garden Wreath quilt. The quilt is divided into a number of blocks and shows appliquéd spray and wreath patterns combined with patchwork maple leaves. (The American Museum in Britain.)*

BELOW RIGHT: *Double Wedding Ring design quilt, c 1940. (The Patchwork Dog and Calico Cat.)*

ABOVE: *Houses and trees hooked rug, c 1825. (The American Museum in Britain.)*

names were used for the quilts themselves when they displayed these repetitive motifs. Other pattern names reflected the effect of the entire quilt instead: Bourgoyne Surrounded, Robbing Peter to Pay Paul, Drunkard's Path, Tumbling Blocks, Lincoln's Platform, Baltimore Bride, Turkey Tracks and Puss-in-the-Corner. Some of these quilts are pieced, others are considered appliquéd if the cutouts were sewn on top, rather than alongside the base material. But the line is sometimes so fine that it takes an expert to differentiate. The rest of us can simply enjoy.

TEXTILES: HOOKED RUGS

Seventeenth-century floors in America were commonly bare earth, packed down and strewn with herbs. Some were even 'polished' by the application of a mixture of oxblood, sand and clay, spread over the earth and then worked in. By the beginning of the 18th century, board floors were more common, sometimes still spread with sand, sometimes left bare. By the mid-18th century, painted and stenciled boards or boards covered with decorated floorcloths – usually canvas – were the fashion. Only in the best homes were the floors dignified with British-made Axminsters or Wiltons, or the even more desirable Oriental carpets. By the early 19th century 'ingrain' (pre-dyed) locally made Kidderminster and Jacquard carpets were widely available, while Axminster and partially mechanized Wilton-style versions were made in America for an affordable, if higher, price.

But the average American homemaker was a thrifty woman, and waste disturbed her. Old clothes and bedclothes – as well as remnants – were recycled as throw rugs, just as off-cuts were put to use in quilts. Shirred and braided rugs were two types that were homemade from the 1820s through the 1850s, but thereafter more hooked rugs were produced than any other kind. Although the technique of hooking was one that had been used for centuries in many parts of the Near East and Europe, it was the Americans and Canadians of the Eastern Seaboard who truly made the craft their own.

Early versions of the hooked rug, beginning around 1820, were backed with homespun linen. After about 1840, the background material tended to be woven cotton or burlap. Cloth strips were fashioned from leftover scraps and a metal hook was used to draw the strips through the coarse weave of the backing to form loops. These loops were either cut or left untrimmed; the longer the strips, whether trimmed or untrimmed, the softer the pile. The more strips made of wool, the stronger the rug; rugs with a substantial proportion of cotton are usually later than woollen examples. A bright hue also is usually an indication of a post-1860 rug made with aniline dyes; early rugs exhibit softer colors, the result of the secondhand materials having been originally colored with natural dyes like cochineal and indigo.

Rugs before about 1870 were home-drawn, the pattern chalked on the background before any looping was begun. The designs were of incredible variety, ranging from geometric to naturalistic to illustrative. In the first category were block and basketweave designs, zigzag rows, *guilloche* – a Victorian chain design with rosette fillers – and fishscale patterns, as well as many others. These seem to be the most usual type for early rugs; in

ABOVE: *Roses with shell border pattern quilt, thought to be from mid 19th century. (The American Museum in Britain.)*

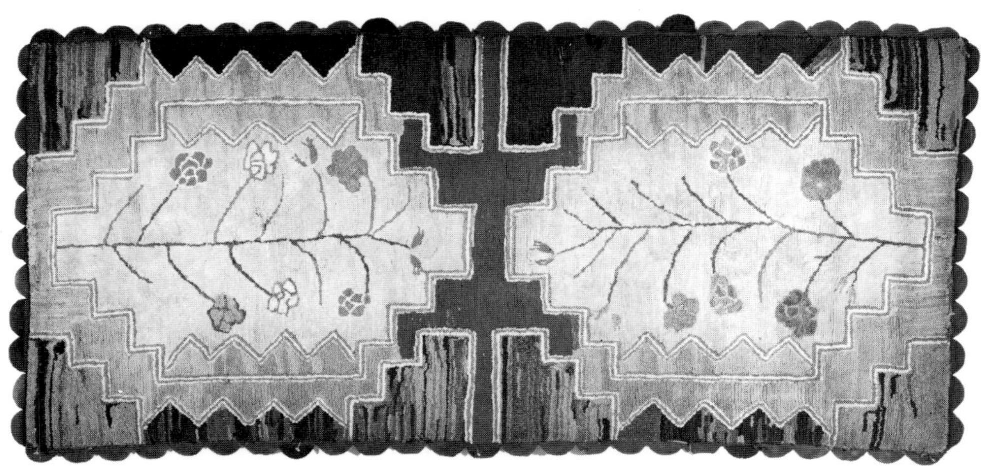

FACING PAGE, TOP: *Firehouse dog rug; cotton on burlap, uncut, late 19th century. (The American Museum in Britain.)*

FACING PAGE, CENTER: *19th-century hooked rug – a style also called 'drawn-in'. (Smithsonian Institution, Washington.)*

FACING PAGE, BELOW: *Hooked and braided rug with design, farmhouse animals; c early 20th century. (Thomas K. Woodard Antiques, New York.)*

RIGHT: *19th-century knitted and braided rug. (Smithsonian Institution, Washington.)*

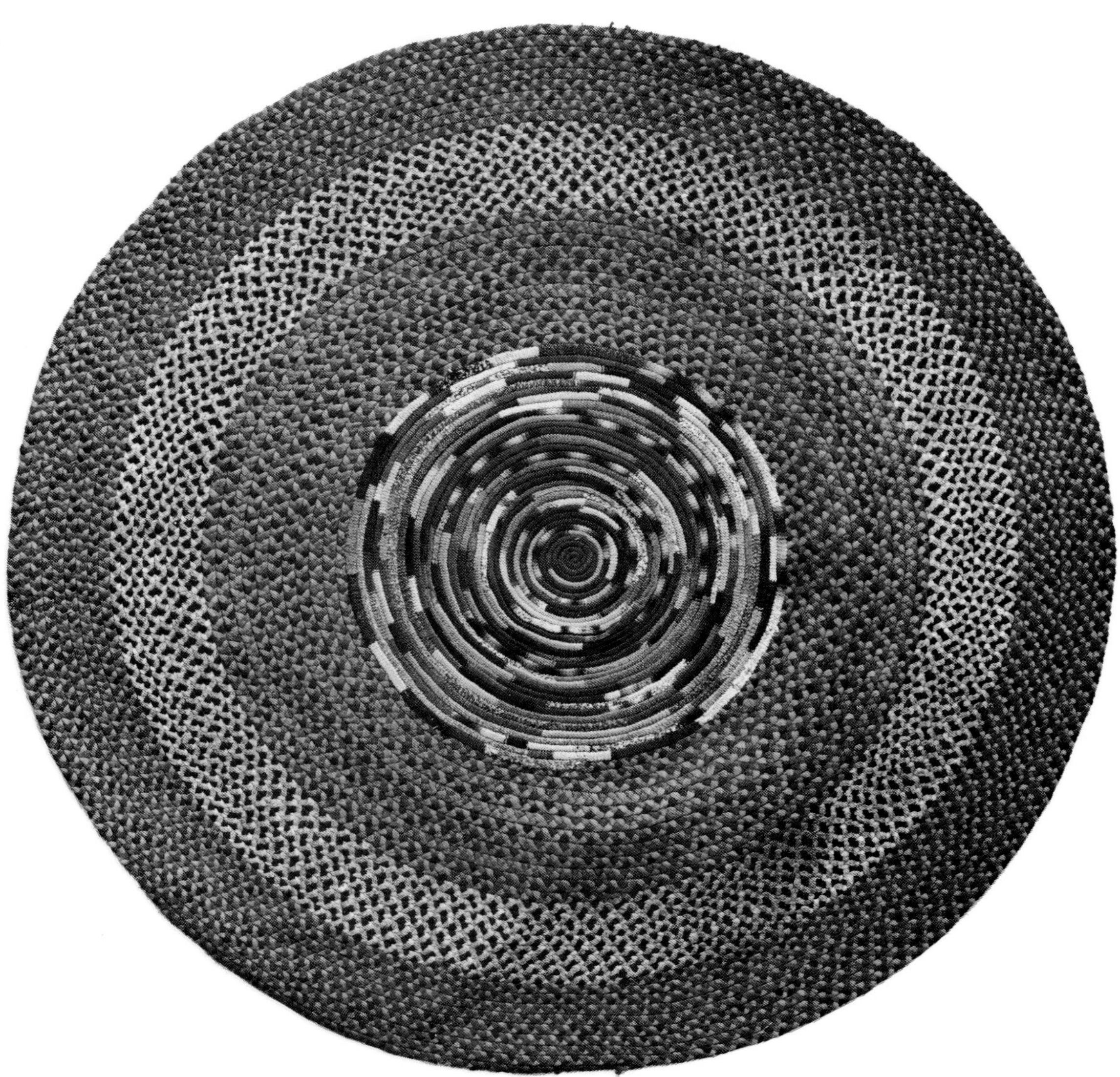

later examples these were sometimes combined with naturalistic or scenic designs, to be used as borders.

Floral designs were consistently popular, the most common being a central spray or bunch of flowers, either loose or confined in a vase or basket, surrounded by a border. Animals ranged from a favorite family pet, like a dog or cat (or two), to more heraldic or exotic creatures such as lions, stags and parrots. The American eagle constituted a particularly patriotic variation that was popular from the 1820s on.

Landscapes and townscapes are rarer but also occur; even scarcer are those examples made by the wives of seafaring men, incorporating shells, knotted ropes, fish or anchors. Rugs with mottoes such as 'God Bless Our Home' or 'Welcome' are usually quite late Victorian.

So proficient did the home craftswoman become that it was not unusual for her to undertake two medium-sized rugs a winter. Hooking bees as well as quilting bees were popular social get-togethers. With the spread of the craft and its acceptance as one of the normal pursuits of the middle-class female, the incentive for commercial development arose. After the Civil War, an invalided Union-soldier-turned-peddler, Edward Sands Frost, began the home-manufacture of stenciled patterns on burlap. His business took off and he continued to produce a wide variety of patterns until the turn of the century. Meanwhile, production had become even more mechanized by the introduction of punch-hooked patterns by Ebenezer Ross of Toledo. Marketing firms including Montgomery Ward offered mail-order patterns.

By the turn of the 20th century, making hooked rugs had become a cottage industry, and whole communities in Canada, New England, and later, the Appalachian Mountains of Tennessee, Kentucky and West Virginia, were turning themselves into rural craft specialists, selling their wares by roadside stands or through representatives. Some of these later cooperative rugs have a folk charm of their own, but often they lack the innovative combinations of color and pattern found on the pre-1900 examples.

C H A P T E R E I G H T

TOYS

Homemade treasures and mechanical marvels that delighted the children of years gone by.

ABOVE: *Carved polychrome revolutionary soldier, c 1785. (Shelburne Museum.)*

ABOVE: *Carved animal toys, c 1850. Artist unidentified; made in Pennsylvania of painted wood. (Abbey Aldrich Rockefeller, Folk Art Center.)*

WOODEN PLAYTHINGS

Making wooden toys to amuse their children was one of the accomplishments of the settler and pioneer. While East Coast gentry could buy the occasional imported toy, even if at great expense, no such opportunity presented itself to most of the American public in the years before their own toy industry was established. Some of these homemade treasures have lasted the years and are today much valued items of craftsmanship, equally sought by toy collectors and by lovers of naïve Americana.

Late 18th- and 19th-century handmade wooden toys include whirligigs, whose flailing arms move in a circular motion alongside the stiffly carved body; windmills, whose light wooden sails spin in the breeze; acrobats who flip over horizontal bars or climb ropes; and clowns who turn somersaults down inclined planes. All of these toys rely on the straightforward rules of physics or the most elemental mechanics in order to work, but are all the more delightful for that.

More static, but just as popular, were the carved dolls, some with their clothes as well as their bodies rendered entirely in wood. Noah's Ark, with its doubled menagerie of beasts, was an extension of this idea and a particular favorite of the young. Especially charming examples, adroitly carved and brightly colored, were produced by Pennsylvania Dutch craftsmen, but examples from New England have their own charm. The Pennsylvania carvers were also responsible for a veritable catalog of

FACING PAGE: *Elephant, made in Pennsylvania c 1850. Carved and painted wood. (Abbey Aldrich Rockefeller, Folk Art Center.)*

BELOW: *Whirligig, made c 1870. (Shelburne Museum.)*

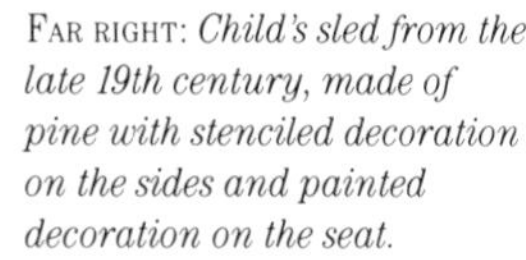

FAR RIGHT: *Child's sled from the late 19th century, made of pine with stenciled decoration on the sides and painted decoration on the seat.*

hand-turned or hand-spun toys in which little human figures whirled, pulled, sawed and hammered until the turning stopped or they ran down. Small toy horses on platforms with wheels were favorites with makers of all regions. But chief among the horsey brigade were those large enough to sit on – the rocking horse.

The rocking horse – the term is used generically, since the majority of American versions are fixed on curved wooden rockers rather than on the parallel-runners mechanism popular in England – was made throughout the 19th and 20th centuries. For most of that time it was the provenance of the amateur craftsman, although in later years small 'factories' of workers were making them, including the Crandalls (see below). Some of the most primitive versions were mere two-dimensional plank creatures with minimal paintwork and rope tails; at the other end of the scale were lifelike, full-bodied animals, with real horsehair manes and tails and realistically dappled coats. Many of the finest were made between 1830 and 1900, but very few of their makers are known.

One of the earliest toy 'factories' was that of William S. Tower of South Hingham, Massachusetts, who founded the Tower Toy Company (later the Tower Guild) in the early 1830s. Makers of wooden toys, dolls and dollhouses, they are best remembered today for their miniature furniture for dollhouses, so lovingly detailed and finished that they have become museum pieces.

In the mid-19th century, the toy-making Crandalls, headed by cousins Jesse A. and Charles A., produced a range of simple mechanism wooden toys. But their several special contributions to toymaking include an early version of the spring-mounted hobby horse that would be so successful in England, and a set of nesting alphabet or spelling blocks – both inventions of Jesse – and the first set of building blocks – the work of Charles. Charles also devised and marketed a toy called 'Pigs in Clover' – the original balls-in-the-maze game. So successful was it that at one point his factory was producing 8,000 per day!

Although wooden toys continued to be made, the appearance of tin and metal toys around 1840 dealt them a severe blow. As the decades passed,

ABOVE: *Two doll's houses with lithographed paper decorations, typical products of the Bliss Manufacturing Company, and dating from 1890–1910. (Margaret Woodbury Strong Museum.)*

wooden versions could claim only a smaller and smaller share of the market. They finally reached the point we are at today, where nostalgia and regard for craftsmanship are the only arguments against a playroom full of plastic rubbish.

TOYS: DOLLS

Dolls, those small mannequins made for little hands to play with, were a late arrival to the pantheon of American-made goods. For over 200 years after the settlement of Jamestown and Plymouth, most dolls came from Europe. They were brought over with the family chattels by immigrants or imported at great expense by grander families for their privileged offspring. Even after 1840 – when several immigrant makers were beginning to ply a small trade in custom-made dolls – and up to the turn of the century, the vast majority of dolls sold in America were either made totally or partially abroad, particularly in Germany.

Those dolls that were made in the colonies – and even a long time after, when the country had become independent – were not mass-produced and are therefore very rare. In addition, their makers strove hard to imitate the fashions prevalent in Great Britain and the Continent, so it is sometimes difficult to pronounce an 18th- or early 19th-century example as indigenous to the United States.

The few really old handmade dolls that have survived were crude affairs – peg dolls; 'bedpost dolls', so-called because of their resemblance to

FACING PAGE: *Cornhusk doll, late 18th century. (The American Museum in Britain.)*

the turned post of a typical colonial bed; wishbone dolls, made from the remnants of a turkey, the inverted 'Y' serving as neck, body and legs, with cloth arms sewn to the covering dress; cornhusk dolls, and dolls made with wooden bodies and heads of dried and preserved apple. A few more sophisticated early 19th-century examples are in special collections. These usually have heads of carved and painted wood, with bodies of either wood or cloth. The 'Dutch' dolls of the mid-19th century conform to this definition.

The first patented American doll only appeared in 1858, the application granted to an immigrant German toy-maker named Ludwig Greiner, who had settled in Philadelphia and worked there from 1840 to 1874. In fact, the patent was only for the head and shoulders, which were manufactured by Greiner from a mixture of white paper, dry Spanish whiting, rye flour and glue, the whole reinforced by an overlay of linen, onto which the features were painted. The heads had molded hairstyles with central partings, and the fashion of the hairstyle provides one of the best clues as to the age of the doll. As for the body, this was usually made by the customer, who would fit it with cloth, wooden or – at best – kid arms attached to the dress.

The introduction of India rubber supplied another medium for doll's heads, and a few surviving dolls from the 1850 to 1870 period possess them. But in fact the hard treatment they received did not marry well with the material and the rubber was prone to crack and decay. It was only after the Civil War, however, that industry was really free to develop into the luxury markets that dolls represented, and factories producing various types were registered in Philadelphia, Boston, Cincinnati and New York, the main port of disembarcation for German immigrants, many of whom, if not doll-makers, possessed traditional skills that were welcome in the trade. Wax, porcelain and composition heads all featured regularly, while in 1873 the first patent for a jointed doll was awarded to New England maker Joel Ellis, few of whose wooden dolls were actually made. Similar patents for 'improved' jointed dolls followed, and in 1881 M.C. Lefferts and W.B. Carpenter opened the Celluloid Manufacturing Company of New York. But it was the 'Can't Break 'Em' dolls of Solomon Hoffman of Brooklyn that opened up the American market to the possibilities of mass-production, and although the new version of composition head devised by Hoffman was not indestructible, it enabled him to open 'The First American Doll Factory', later incorporated into the American Doll and Toy Manufacturing Company. It was one of these heads that was used for the first American copyrighted doll – Billiken – made between 1909 and 1912 by the E.I.

RIGHT: *Painted papier mâché doll, 19th century. (The American Museum in Britain.)*

Horsman Company of New York City, which also produced the first advertising dolls – the 'Campbell Kids' made under license from the famous soup company.

In the meantime, the old-fashioned homemade cloth doll had gone commercial. 'Mammy' dolls and 'rag' dolls had been popular for many years in the South and North, cut to supplied patterns and filled by the customer. But in 1873 Mrs. Izannah Walker of Central Falls, Rhode Island, obtained a patent for making rag dolls with a double-molded cotton and wadding head, joined to bodies of muslin. Later, from the 1890s through the 1920s, Martha Chase of Pawtucket, Rhode Island, moved the technique up-market, producing dolls portraying fairy tale and literary characters, as well as famous people. These Chase dolls are today highly sought-after. Perhaps the most famous of the rag dolls, however, were the Raggedy Ann and Andy dolls, first patented in 1915 by the creator of the eponymous books. Their distinctive red yarn hair, shoe-button eyes, pinafore (Ann) and sailor stripes (Andy) turned them into a childhood classic (now produced by the Knickerbocker Toy Company).

The antithesis to the simplicity of the rag doll was the fascination with human mimicry implicit in all the moving, crying and talking dolls that appeared as the years marched on. The first 'walking doll' was patented in 1862; its complicated and ugly machinery was hidden beneath wide crinoline skirts. In 1877 came a walking and crying doll; in 1881, a singing doll. This last was an expensive

LEFT: *Cloth doll by Ludwig Greiner, 1858–72. (Margaret Woodbury Strong Museum.)*

item, with long, curling hair sprouting from a wax head and a kid body, on which was printed the name of the song she could warble.

Up to and including the early decades of the 20th century, children had been content with dolls that looked like young women or, at best, children their own age. The vogue for the baby doll took off with the Bye-Lo Baby, designed by Grace Storey Putnam in 1922 and said to be modeled on a real baby only a few days old. It was a cooperative effort, with the bisque heads made in Germany, the cloth body made and the assembly of the dolls accomplished by K & K Toy Company of New York, and the distribution handled by George Borgfeldt and Co. Within two years, however, the German heads were replaced with all-American wood-pulp composition heads, and a year later with celluloid heads. Some wooden heads and a few wax prototypes have also been found.

The 1920s saw advertising dolls, taking their lead from the Campbell Kids, become an important force in the toy market. Dolls based on cartoon characters also appeared in the 1920s, to reach their peak in the 1930s and 1940s with the Disney-licensed dolls. These were also the big days for film star dolls – Shirley Temple being the queen of them all – and even dolls based on unseen radio stars. By the 1940s plastics were being used in doll manufacture, leading to a general lowering of standards and styling, while the introduction of vinyl in the late 1950s has meant a return to better modeling, if not inspired design.

ABOVE LEFT: *Clockwork hoop toy, made by Althof Bergmann c 1870–80. (Bill Holland Collection. Reproduced courtesy of New Cavendish Books.)*

ABOVE RIGHT: *Clockwork figure of General Grant, made by Ives and Blakeslee c 1877. (Margaret Woodbury Strong Museum.)*

TOYS: METAL AND MECHANICAL TOYS

The first tin toys appeared in the 1840s. At first, the simple die-stamped shapes, crimped or riveted together, followed the pattern set by the wooden variety. Chief among the companies making them were the Philadelphia Tin Toy Manufactory and George W. Brown and Company of Connecticut. The tin toys were light, versatile and cheap, but they were not very resilient. As if in uncomplicated answer to the problem, cast-iron toys began to be made in the late 1860s, although they were not made in great numbers until the 1880s. They were certainly solid and sturdy, but they were heavy and most could not be wound by hand or easily carried about by little people. Instead iron toys took the form of static playthings – miniature stoves like Mommy's with little pots and pans to match or simple slot banks – or pull-along wagons, dogs, horses and carts, fire engines and circus animals on wheels. Sometime in the late 1860s, George Brown's tin-making firm joined forces with J. & E. Stevens, the first major iron toy company, eventually becoming known as the American Toy Company. With the invention of spring-action toys in the early 1870s, it was in an enviable commercial position and became one of the principal makers of the new mechanical banks.

A penny in the hand of a clown – or of a corrupt politician, in the case of the 'Tammany Hall Bank' – would be popped into his mouth or dropped into

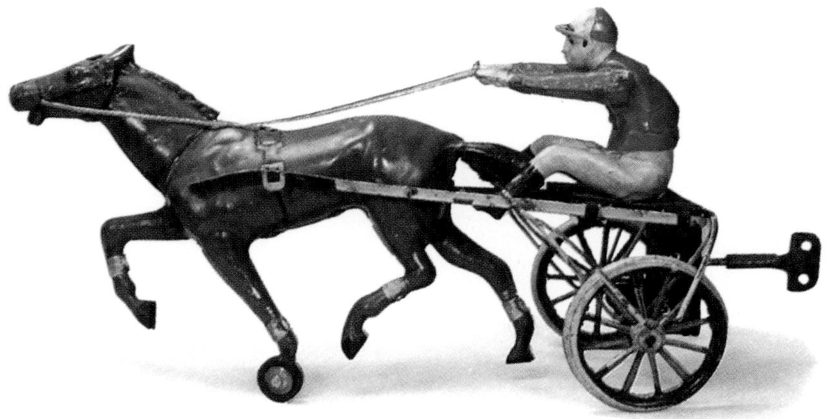

his portmanteau (as in the 'Uncle Sam' bank); placed in the hammer of a cannon or breech of a rifle it would be 'fired' into a target; dropped into the paw of a monkey it would be thrown into the lion's mouth, while a mother bird 'chirped' as she 'fed' her babies a copper coin. The heyday of these banks was between 1870 and 1910; incredibly, fewer than a dozen firms had a share of the (spring) action, which at present count numbers over 600 patterns!

Spring-action toys were really a preliminary to the clockwork movement, which was introduced into tin toys at the same time. Winding up the toy and letting the mechanism play down enabled toy people to walk and dance, horses to 'trot,' carriages to roll, bicycles to be ridden, trains to 'locomote', and eventually, in the 1900s, cars to be 'driven' by tiny goggled drivers. Music boxes too benefited from the simple new device. The few clockwork iron toys that were manufactured are particularly sought-after.

Among the notable makers of clockwork toys were J. & E. Stevens; Althof, Bergman & Company; and Edward R. Ives, the first toymaker in the United States to make a model railway, complete with tracks, that actually ran. Even when they were made, many of these clockwork and spring-action toys – particularly the banks – were often as popular with adults as with children. 'Tammany Hall', 'Uncle Sam' and such political banks could even be considered the first toys for bored executives!

TOP: *Three clockwork walking dolls patented by Arthur E. Hotchkiss in 1875. (Margaret Woodbury Strong Museum.)*

ABOVE LEFT: *Hand-painted tinplate trotter, designed to run in circles and powered by a simple clockwork motor. Thought to be of late 19th-century manufacture. (The Lost Street Museum, Ross-on-Wye, UK.)*

C H A P T E R N I N E

WOOD-CARVING

A traditional rendering of respected forms, embracing Indian chiefs, holy guardians and the American eagle.

ABOVE: *Cigar store Indian princess, 6′1″ (183cm) in height, 19th century. (The American Museum in Britain.)*

LEFT: *Wood carving of a man on horseback; painted, c 1880s. (American Folk Art.)*

LARGE WOOD FIGURES

The craft of American figurehead carving extended from the early days of the Republic through 1880, a span of 100 years. It was a form of sculpture that inspired American artisans to a particularly high degree. The opportunity for carving patriotic and nationalistic motifs was not lost on them; their delight in their native Americana was given full reign. Ship owners and their families were immortalized as well as Indian chiefs and princesses, admirals and generals, and the always popular Lady Liberty. Famous historical figures like George Washington, Benjamin Franklin, Henry Ward Beecher and Andrew Jackson adorned the fore of ships. A dark charmer fronted the *Creole* of 1847, while a Negro mascot of the Union Army saw out his service on a *c*1864 naval rigger.

Eagles were used both as figureheads and sternboards – usually painted or gilded to set off the eye and beak against the brown wood feathers. Many decorated the pilot houses of tugboats, others spread their wings above the far grander decks of Mississippi paddleboats. The eagle was combined with a shield or flag on some occasions; on others, the wing spread took up all the available wood.

The typical American figurehead was more thrusting and erect than its British counterpart. Like an intrepid explorer in the new country, it peered forward with unclouded eye into the distance. That the carving of such mystic characters was a respected employment is attested to by the caliber of many of the carvers, intinerant though many were. Among them were Samuel McIntire (1757–1811), of Salem, Massachusetts, who was well-known as an architectural carver and academic wood-carver of monumental busts of such worthies as Voltaire, George Washington and John Winthrop; and Laban S. Beecher of Boston, the most celebrated ship carver of the first part of the 19th century, author of the figurehead for the *Constitution*, the most famous ship in American history. There were many figureheads that can only be attributed to a known area of carvers – Essex, Connecticut or New Bedford, Massachusetts, for instance – or to the combined artistry of a group, like Hastings &

ABOVE LEFT: *Carved eagle. 42" (115cm) tall; made 1850. (American Folk Art).*

ABOVE RIGHT: *Wooden plover decoy by John Delby, Long Island 1890. (American Folk Art.)*

FACING PAGE, TOP: *'Armstrong' featherweight decoy c 1900. This type of decoy was very popular in Illinois. Painted canvas sewn over an excelsior body. (The American Museum in Britain.)*

FACING PAGE, CENTER: *Large wooden decoy duck of unknown date. (American Museum in Britain.)*

FACING PAGE, BELOW: *The texturing of this decoy duck combined with realistic painting give it a lifelike quality. (The American Museum in Britain.)*

Gleason of Boston, William Gleason & Sons of Boston, or Dodge & Son of New York.

Like McIntire, many carvers worked in more than one field. The academic carver from Philadelphia, William Rush, began by producing figureheads and, later, cigar-store Indians, and Thomas V. Brooks (see below) turned from the sea to the weed, carving tobacconists' figures for over 35 years. These three-dimensional salesmen, made particularly for tobacconists, can be traced as far back as *c*1825, when a slave named Job is said to have made an Indian for a tobacconist in Freehold, New Jersey. Some earlier, flat boards, painted on both sides, almost certainly served much the same purpose.

The main period of activity began with the opening of John L. Cromwell's carving shop in 1831, in Lower Manhattan, but it was not until his apprentice, Thomas V. Brooks, opened his factory in 1847, producing over 200 a year, that the big-city street figure was on the way to becoming a truly national fixture. As late as 1937, 585 were still in use in 42 states.

Artisan-businessmen like Cromwell and one Mr Caspari of Baltimore turned the making of these figures into a form of mass-production. A few individual carvers, like Samuel A. Robb, another fugitive from marine carving who produced figures for Brooks from 1860, and Julius Theodore Melchers of Detroit are names to be reckoned with, but for the most part the craftsmen are anonymous. The work took the form of four basic types: Chiefs, Squaws and Pocahontas; Blackamoors or Pompeys; and White Men (and, rarely, Women). The latter range from historical figures like Sir Walter Raleigh (the discoverer of tobacco), to literary personalities such as Mr Pickwick and Captain Jinks of the Horse Marines to ethnic or national stock characters like the Turk, the Scotsman and Uncle Sam. While these creatures of advertising are today highly collectible – and in many cases, museum pieces – they are still more accessible than the larger-than-life and much rarer ship's figureheads.

WOOD-CARVING: DECOYS

The carving of decoys is one of the oldest crafts in the United States. Long before the Revolution, settlers in small towns and villages, as well as backwoodsmen, were turning out waterbirds from blocks of cedar, cypress, balsa and pine – or any other available, if less common wood, such as holly or hawthorne. From the period of the Civil War

onward, the styling became more and more eloquent, if still very much in the folk tradition. The classic collector's period stretches from this time to about 1920, when the era of the individual carver was superseded by factory-made birds.

The variety of birds carved encompasses the vast wildfowl and shorebird population of our beaches, banks and lakes. The loving renditions range from all species of ducks, drakes and geese – which today forms the usual hunter's quarry – to yellowlegs, plovers and curlews, which were much pursued in the 19th century (in the curlew's case almost to extinction). Some of the latter birds also served as 'confidence decoys', deployed to create a peaceful scene so that the more desirable species would settle. The rare swan decoys fall into both camps, since until 1913 they were legal quarry. The representation of the birds fell into three distinct types: the familiar floating variety, used for the ducks and geese; the 'stick-up' more common for the elongated shorebirds and the 'flatty' – a cutout silhouette used particularly in the Cape Cod region, often for inland birds as a kind of scarecrow.

While decoys were carved for use on Michigan lakes, and for as far south as the Carolinas and as far north as Maine, the unquestioned center of decoy carving was the Massachusetts coast, particularly around Cape Cod. Some of the great carvers of the area include Captain Osgood (*fl*1870–80), William Henry Weston (*fl*1890s), Joe Lincoln (*fl*1870–1910) and Elmer Crowell (*fl*1900–15). Connecticut boasted Albert Laing (*fl*1860–80) and Charles 'Shang' Wheeler (*fl*1920–30), while Nathan Cobb (*fl*1870–90) and Ira Hudson (*fl*1910–20) were important names among the many carvers who worked on the islands off the Virginia coast. Although, in general, the rise of the 'decoy factory' spelled the end for the handicraft, the products of the Dodge Decoy Factory (begun 1880) and the Mason Decoy Factory (*fl*1899–26) of Detroit, Michigan, have become collector's items in their own right.

WOOD-CARVING: SANTOS AND BULTOS

The influence of the Franciscan fathers on the arts and crafts of the Southwest was enormous. Not only did the fervor of their Catholicism transfer itself to carvings and folk sculptures, particularly those produced by New Mexican artisans, but the handicrafts taught by the missions – how to carve in stone and wood, work in tin and silver, make plaster, or use paints in the Spanish manner – were put toward translating the religious pictures of the peasant mind into *santos*, solid images for the greater glory of God.

RIGHT: *Virgin & Nino bulto from the early 19th century. The full skirt is made of animal skin, gessoed and painted. Nino is attached with a thong. (The American Museum in Britain.)*

FACING: *Captain Jenks large carved figure, c 1879. Made to stand outside an outfitters' or tobacconists' shop. (Newark Museum.)*

At first the priests produced some of the handiwork themselves, at the same time instructing the local craftsmen. These early pieces were sometimes signed; the names of Father Garcia (*fl*1747–79) Father Pereyro (*fl*1798–1818) are among those that can be traced. Painted on pine or cottonwood panels treated with gesso (wet plaster), their works are known as *retablos* and were used to decorate the churches. In the next generation, both priests and lay artists attempted to reproduce the lively charm of the earlier *retablos,* but the versions that appeared after the first decades of the 19th century lacked that vital spark.

Instead, the *santeros* (the generic name applied to the makers and repairers of religious images) turned their talents toward making small shrines for private homes, a sort of Christian version of the Roman *lares*, or holy guardian, to extend his protection and intercession for the family living there. These shrines were now three-dimensional statuettes or groups, now more usually made of cottonwood roots. Called *bultos*, they were covered in gesso and painted in tempera, sometimes including material to give them a realistic touch.

ABOVE: *Pedro y Pablo bulto, made in New Mexico; date unknown. (Richard Worthen Galleries; Robert Reck Photography.)*

FACING PAGE: *The Archangel Michael. (Robert Reck Photography.)*

The styles of the little shrines vary according to the region of origin. In New Mexico, those of the Santa Cruz school are tall and lean with austere decoration; those of Cordova are finely carved, with expressive features and hands in the manner of the older *retablos.* These are thought to be the work of Miguel or José Raphael Aragon. Another group, known as the Mora *bultos*, date from the Civil War period and are overtly stylized, with dotted, painted eyebrows and lashes and small black-booted feet.

While the largest number of *bultos* are the legacy of the New Mexican (including the Arizona/Texas regions) mission influence, a respectable number have also been preserved in the 21 missions of California.

C H A P T E R T E N

FIREARMS

How the West was won: conquering the vast American continent with Kentucky rifles and Colt .45s.

ABOVE: *Varnished walnut grip derringer with hard rubber, pearl and ivory. (Remington Museum).*

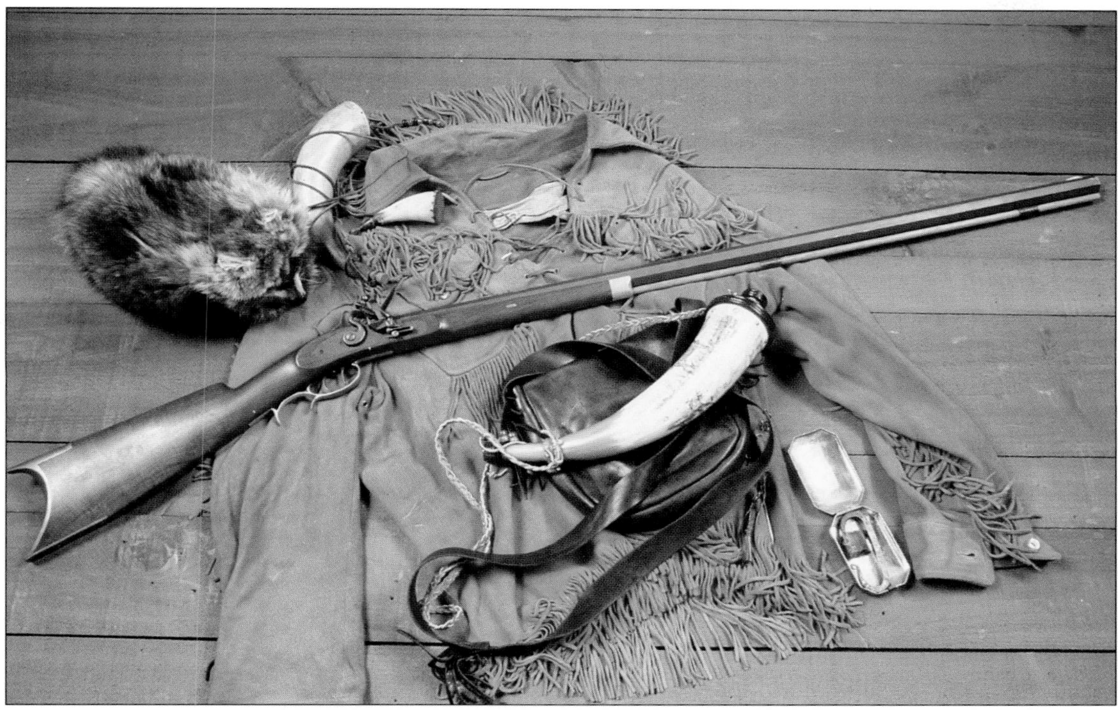

In the popular mind, the conquest of the original colonies and the opening of the American West has always been linked, in an almost romantic partnership, with the development of the gun. The Pilgrims stand on Plymouth Rock, blunderbuss under their arms (a disappointing anachronism, since the blunderbuss was not common in England until the mid-17th century); Daniel Boone, Davy Crockett and James Fenimore Cooper's Natty Bumppo aim their trusty Kentucky rifles through the undergrowth; countless sheriffs in dusty sun-baked streets twirl their Colt .45s in the inevitable showdown, and fancy cardsharps on the Mississippi riverboats polish their pearl-handled derringers before concealing them in their frock-coat pocket. Although the reality was less glamorous, it is probably true that without the challenges – animal and human – presented by the vastness of the American continent, the history of firearms would be a far different one.

Although the discovery and early settlement of America coincided with the exploitation of gunpowder and firearms in Western Europe, it took some time before the colonists began to make their own mark in the field. It was during the Seven Years' War that American gunsmiths were first encouraged to make their own guns rather than import them, since the British troops were thwarted from receiving needed supplies by blockade and naval battles. By the time of the Revolution, there were enough capable gunsmiths in the colonies to keep the Minutemen, the Green Mountain Boys and their like well equipped, their muskets repaired. The muskets and pistols they produced, however, were very much in the mold of those carried by their red-coated enemy, but for one noteworthy exception: the Kentucky (or Pennsylvania or Lancaster Valley) rifle.

This colonial firearm was first made in the early 18th century by the German settlers of the area, who patterned it on the *Jaeger* or hunter's rifle of their homeland. To meet the requirements of their new country they increased the octagonal barrel to 40 or 45 in (102 to 114 cm) in length, decreased the caliber, and improved the firing efficiency by loading the bullets in greased linen patches (kept in the recessed patchbox in the stock) that were discarded as the bullet left the barrel. These guns were also distinguished by their 'curly' maple or walnut stocks, with the most elegant examples having simple brass inlay or carving. The Pennsylvania rifle reached its apogee by the mid- to late 18th century, and by the 1790s had become excessively decorated, with a more sharply sloping butt.

By the 1820s, the flintlock had replaced the percussion cap and the long rifle was shortened and modified to become the plainsman's companion, a common sight on the road West blazed by Lewis

ABOVE LEFT: *Reproduction of an early Remington flintlock. (Remington Museum.)*

BELOW LEFT: *Beals Navy revolver, c 1860–62. Single action, .36 caliber, walnut grip; barrel marked 'Manufactured by Remington Ilion, New York'. (Remington Museum.)*

OVERLEAF: *New Model Pocket Revolver, c 1863, .31 caliber, walnut varnished grip with pearl and ivory. (Remington Museum.)*

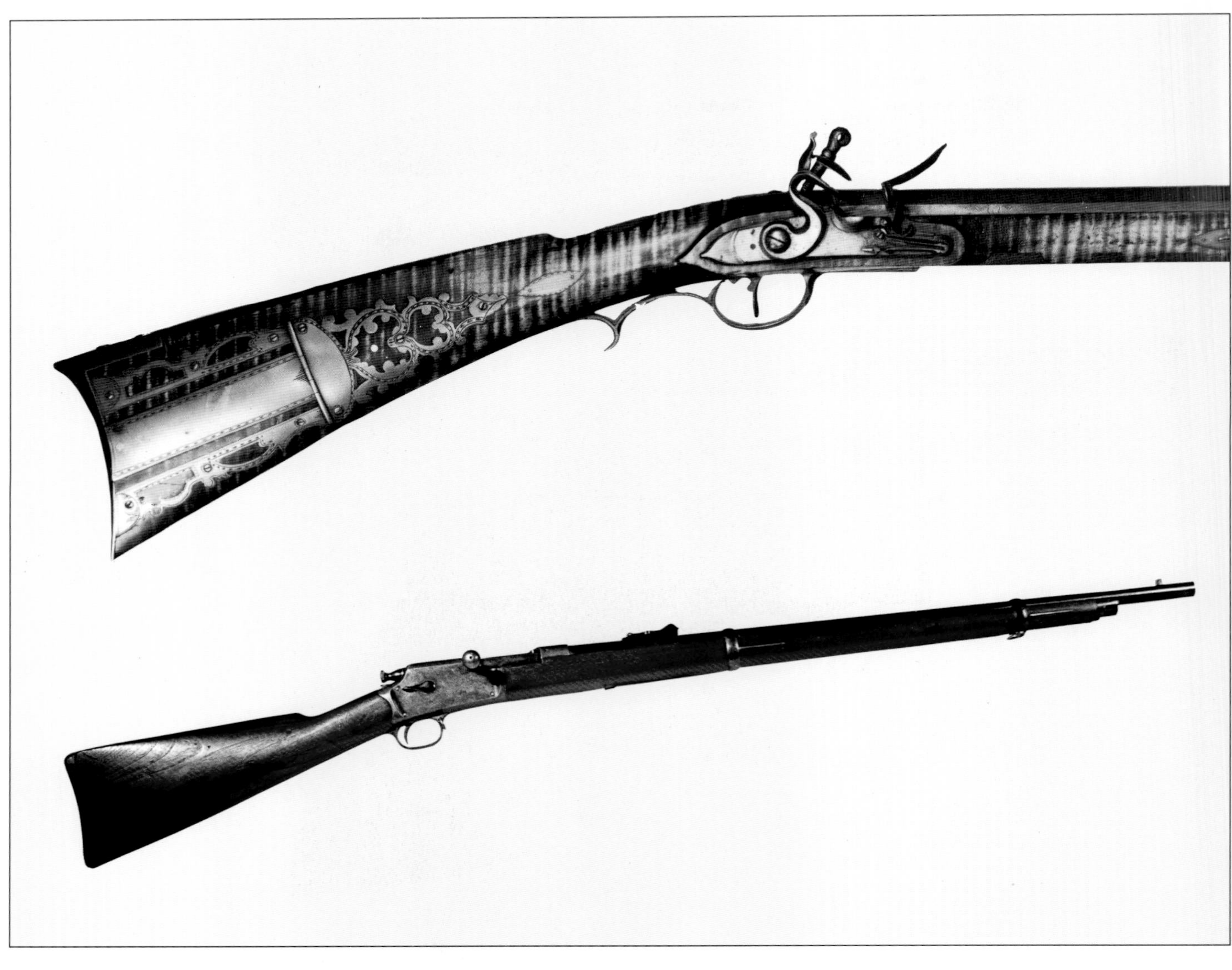

ABOVE: *The Winchester-Hotchkiss rifle M1883 was the first American bolt-action service rifle.*

TOP: *Kentucky rifle with characteristic maplewood stock inlaid with pierced and engraved brass and silver plaques. Made c 1800. (Christie's, New York.)*

and Clark. The two variations are usually distinguished as the 'Kentucky' rifle, made in the Appalachian region, and the 'Plains' rifle, made in Kansas and St. Louis, where the premier firm was Hawken Brothers.

But handguns are the area in which the American contribution had international repercussions. An early version of the revolver was devised by Captain Artemas Wheeler of Concord, Massachusetts (no plans or examples survive, however), but it was not until 1818 that the American gunsmith Elisha Collier of Boston, an erstwhile associate of the Captain, patented a flintlock revolver in London, where he had taken his business. It had an automatic priming device and a barrel-locking system that insured that the revolving chamber did not allow gas to escape on the moment of firing, thus eliminating the risk of explosion. But despite these radical innovations, his revolver was not a commercial success.

It took another American, Samuel Colt, to take up and develop the idea, gaining patents in both England and France in 1835 and in the United States in 1836 for his percussion revolver – the prototype of all subsequent revolvers, up to the present day. His first factory was established in Paterson, New Jersey, in 1836, and it produced pistols, shotguns, rifles and carbines – all with revolving cylinders. But the firm went bust and the factory was sold. Today the 'Paterson Colt' guns, particularly the .28 caliber revolvers, are prime collector's items. It was only in 1847, after Captain Samuel Walker of the Texas Rangers assisted in producing a modified design (and political expediency lent a helping hand by way of the Mexican-American War), that Colt was able to gain a government contract for a thousand of his pistols. He opened another factory – and never looked back. These 'Walker Colts' were very unwieldy and crudely made, but they did hard service in the Army. They are among the most highly prized of all Colt models.

Several more Colt revolvers followed, notably the 'Navy' .36 caliber revolver of 1851 – the most popular of all Colt percussion-cap military revolvers – an 1860 revision of the Colt .44 caliber of 1848, which became a popular Union model during the Civil War, and in 1857 the first solid-frame Colt

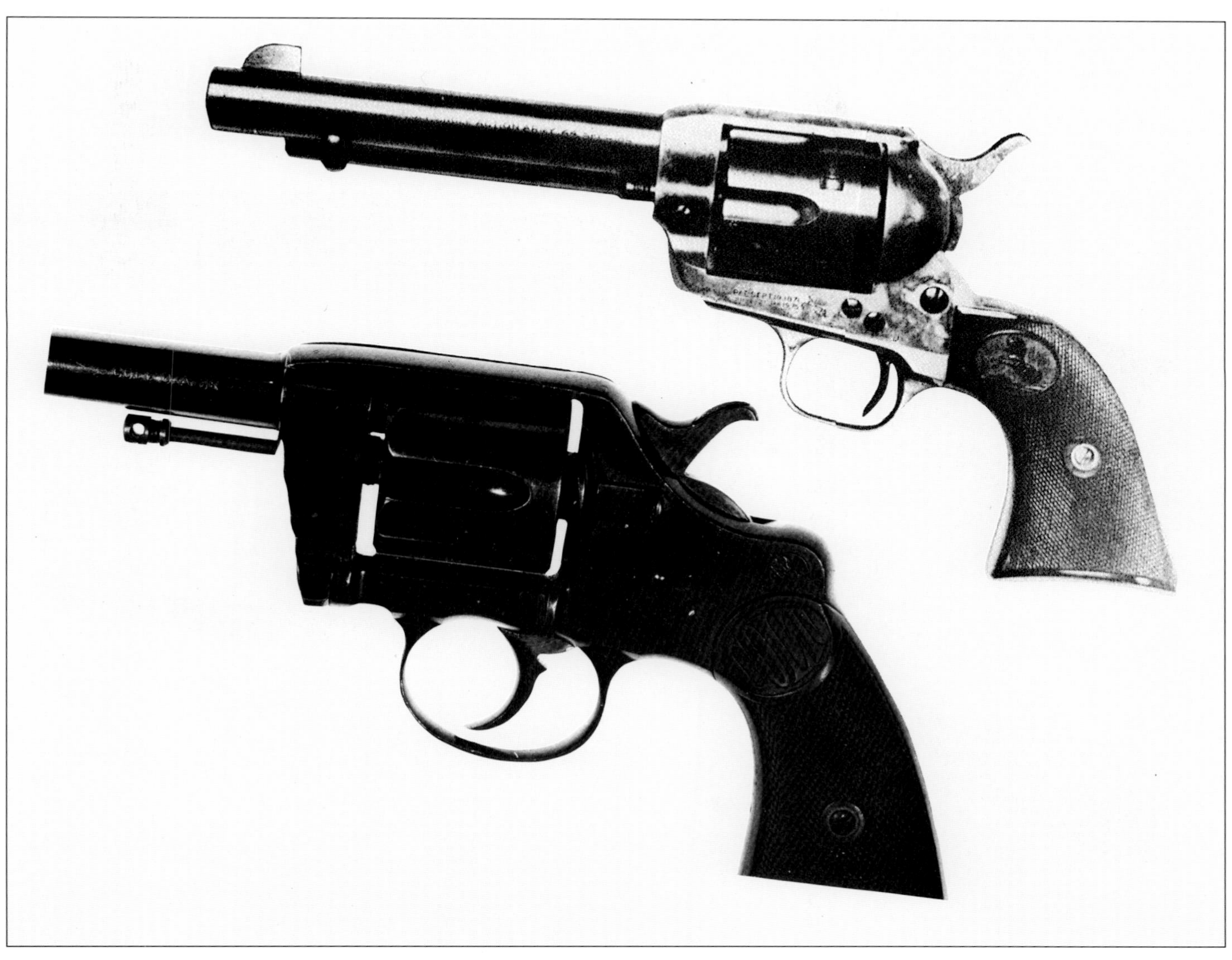

revolver. This last was designed by Elisha K. Root, factory superintendent and later president of the company. It revolutionized revolver production throughout the world.

The most famous Colt handgun, the 'Peacemaker', immortalized in scores of classic Western films, was not made until 1873, 11 years after Colt's death. This 'six-shooter' was available in calibers ranging from .22 to .476, but it was the 'Colt .45' that still strikes the richest chord in Western legend and lore.

Meanwhile other gunsmiths were making a mark in the annals of firearms. Henry Deringer of Philadelphia began specializing in short-barreled pocket pistols with large calibers. Fired with percussion caps, they ranged in size from a mere 3¼ in (9.5 cm) to 9 in(23 cm), but boasted calibers from .33 to .51. These small power-packed weapons became immensely popular as a gentleman's accessory, particularly in the South and West. It spawned many imitators, and the term 'deringer' (or, more commonly, 'derringer') became synonymous with any small gun, not necessarily one manufactured by, or even like those made by, Deringer himself. The derringer gained national notoriety when it was identified as the weapon used by John Wilkes Booth, the 'gentleman actor', to assassinate President Abraham Lincoln in 1864.

Eliphalet Remington, Jr, began by making both flint and percussion-cap rifles, but in 1849 he began working on a revolver. By 1856 he had refined it and, in 1860, like Colt, achieved a government contract to supply the Union Army. Over 128,000 Remington revolvers were issued to Union troops and other government stores during the four years of the war.

The fortunes of the great Winchester rifle were also assisted by the outbreak of the Civil War. Horace Smith and Daniel Wesson had been working on repeating pistols and rifles since 1831. But it was not until the war that the design of the earlier lever-action Jennings rifle was effectively modified by the two men and sufficient numbers produced to make the Smith and Wesson rifle as popular as the Colt revolver. It went on to face even tougher service in the Indian Wars, Sheep and Cattle Wars, and other major and minor skirmishes that punctuated the way westard.

ABOVE: *Colt .38 'New Army' revolver of 1893, one of the first solid-frame side-opening revolvers.*

TOP: *The famous Frontier, or Peacemaker, in .45 caliber.*

INDEX

Italic page numbers refer to illustrations

A
Adler and Sullivan 57
Affleck, Thomas 11, 28
Alford, Arba 15
Allis, Captain John 38-9
Althof, Bergmann & Company *156* 157
Amelung, John Frederick 94
American Doll and Toy Manufacturing Company 153
American Flint Glass *100, 101*
American Pottery Company 125
American Toy Company 156
Amish sect *142*
andirons 83, *86*
Aragon, José Raphael 165
Aragon, Miguel 165
Art Nouveau *19*, 75
Arts and Crafts movement
ceramics 130, *130, 131*, 132, *132, 133*
desks *58*
furniture 56-8, *57, 58, 59*
glass, 73, 109, *110*, 111-12, *111, 112, 113, 114, 115*, 117-8, *117, 118, 119*
Mission furniture 58
Roycrofters 58
silver 75, *75, 76*, 77, *77*
Avon Pottery 130

B
Bakewell, John 99, 104
Bakewell plant *90*
Bartlam, Joseph 124
Bassett, Francis 79
Bassett, Frederick 79
Bauer and Hill 57
beakers 67, 68-9
beds 33-4, *33, 34*, 36
bed hangings 33, 34, *35*, 137
field 34
four-posters 34, *34*
French bed 34
high-post 33, 34
sleigh 34
testers 34
trundle 33
Beecher, Laban S. 159
Bell family (potters) 122
Belter, John Henry 15, 18, *19*, 34, *36*
Bennington pottery 125, 129
Berlin woolwork 137
Bible boxes 36, *36*
Birmingham Glass Works *102*
Black, James 72
Black, John 72
Blanck, Jurian, Jr *67*
bleeding bowls 69
Bliss Manufacturing Company *152*
Bloomingdale Flint Glass Works 99
Bock, William, & Brother 129
Boelen, Jacob *68*, 70
Bonnin, Gouse 129
Bonnin and Morris *126, 127*
book boxes 36
bookcases and bureau-bookcases 30, 31, *31*, 33, *33*
Borgfeldt, George, and Co. 155
Boston and Sandwich Glass Company *97*, 104, 105, *107, 108*
Bowen, Samuel 127
boxes 29, 36
Shaker 47, *48*
Bradford, Cornelius 79
Bradford, William 79
Brasher, Ephraim 72
brass 81, 83, *86*
breakfront 28
Brewster chairs, 7, 11
Bristol Clock Company 64
Britannia ware 81
Bromley, William 129-30
bronze *85*
Brooklyn Flint Glass Works 99
Brooks, Thomas V. 160
Brown, George W., and Company 156
Brown, J.C. 64
Buckley, Oliver 86-7
bultos 163, 165, *165*
Burnap, Daniel 61, 62
Burnham, Benjamin 30
Burt, Benjamin 72
Butler family (toleware painters) 87

C
cabriole legs 34
California bungalow style 58
candlestands 22, *24*
candlesticks 49
caned furniture 11, 17, *17*, 18, 33
Carder, Frederick *110*, 118
'Carolingian' style 11, 33-4, 69
Carpen, Solomon, Bros *19*
Carpenter, W.B. 153
Cartlidge, Charles, & Company 129
carving *see* WOOD-CARVING
Caspari, Mr 160
caudle cups 68-9, 69
Celluloid Manufacturing Company 153
ceramics 120-33
Arts and Crafts movement 130, *130, 131*, 132, *132, 133*
commemorative and patriotic subjects 125, 126
gilding 129
porcelain clocks 64
transfer-printed 125
chairs 11-20
balloon back 18
bentwood 15
Brewster 7, 11
buffalo horn and deer antler 15
canework 11, 17, *17*
Carvers 11
Hitchcock *14*
ladderback 11
mass-produced 15
mushroom hand rests 11
rocking 15, *47*
rush-seated 11, 15
Shaker 46, 47, *47*
turkey-work 11, 17
upholstered 11, 17-20
Wainscot 11
Windsor 11, *12*
wing *14*, 17, *19, 20*
X-seat 12
chandeliers 83
Chase, Martha 154
Chelsea Ceramic Art Works (Chelsea Pottery) 132
Cheney, Benjamin 61
Cheney Brothers 61
chests 36, 38-9
blanket *10*, 26, 38, *39*
chest of drawers 26, 28, 29, 42, 47, *47, 48*
chest-on-chest 29, 30
chest-on-stand 26
Connecticut 26, 38
doughboys 45
dower 39, 44-5, *45*, 51
Hadley 26, 38-9, *38*
Hartford 38
highboys 26, *26*, 28-9, *28*, 30
hope 26, 39
lowboys 26, 28, *29, 30*
Mary Pease chest 39
Pennsylvania Dutch 44-5, *45*
Shaker 46, 47, *47, 48*
Sunflower 38
Chicago School 56-7
Chippendale style
beds 34, *34*
chairs, 11, *14, 15, 19*
daybeds *36*
desks *27, 29*, 30, *32*
highboys 28
sofas 17
tables *21*, 22, *23, 24, 25, 26*
Cincinatti Art Pottery 130
clocks 60-5
banjo 63, *63*
box-on-box 64
brass movements 61, 64
case-on-case 64
Federal style *60*
garnitures 64, *64*
girandole 63
Gothic steeple 64
long-case (grandfather) 61-2, *61*
lyre 63
mass-produced 62, 63, 64
Massachussets shelf clock 64
mirror clocks *62*
O.G. 64
ormolu *64*
painted and decorative finishes *61*
papier-mâché 64
pillar-and-scroll 64
porcelain 64
shelf 63, *63*, 64, *64, 65*
steel springs 64
stencilled decoration 64, *64*
Tiffany *61, 64*
verre eglomisé 42
wag-on-the-wall 62, 63
wall clocks 62, 63, *63*
wooden movements 61, 62, 63, 64, *65*
clockwork toys *156*, 157, *157*
Cobb, Nathan 162
Coburn, John 71
coffeepots and services
ceramic *121*
silver 73-5, *73, 74*
tinware 85, *86*
Collier, Elisha 170
Colt, Samuel 170-1, *171*
commemorative items
ceramics 125, 126
figureheads and shop signs 159, 160
glass 100, *102*, 103-4, *103, 104, 105*
mourning pictures 137
Coney, John 68, 69, 71, *72*
confessionals
Southwestern style 49, 51
Connecticut Glass Works *105*
Copeland, Joseph 79
copper, 81, 83
couches 17
court cupboards *37*, 39, 41
Crandalls toys 151
creamware 124-5, *124*
crewelwork 34, 137

Crolyas (Crolius) pottery 122
Cromwell, John L. 160
Crowell, A. Elmer 7, 162
cup and cover *67*
cupboards
  corner *39*
  court *37*, 39, 41
  Pennsylvania Dutch 45
  press 39, 41
  schranks *43*, 45
  Shaker 46, *48*
  Southwestern style 51, *52*, *54*
  trasero 51, *52*, 56
cupping bowls 69
Curtis, Lemuel 63
Cushing & White 83

D
Daly, Matthew A. *130*
Danforth, Joseph 70
Danforth, Thomas 79
Day, Benjamin 79
daybeds, 17, 33-4, *36*, *46*
decoy ducks 160, *160*, *161*
Dedham Pottery 132
Deringer, Henry 171
desks 29-31
  blockfront 30-1
  bookcase-secretary 31, *31*
  desk-on-frame 30
  kneehole *29*, 31
  slant front *29*, 30
  slope front *29*, 30
  Wooton's Patent, *31*, *32*
  writing stand 30
Directoire style 31, 33
Disbrowe, Nicholas 38
Dodge & Son 160
Dodge Decoy Factory 162
dolls 152-5
  bedpost 152-3
  clockwork *157*
  cloth 153, 154, *155*
  composite 153
  cornhusk 153, *153*
  Dutch 153
  jointed 153
  papier-mâché *154*
  peg 152
  porcelain 153
  rag 154
  rubber 153
  wax 153
  wishbone 153
  wooden 149, 151, 153
dollshouses 151, *152*
Dominick & Haff 77
doughboys 45
Duché, Andrew 127
Duché, Antoine 127
Dummer, Jeremiah 68
Dunlap, Samuel II 28
Dwight, Timothy 68
Dyottville Glass Works 104

E
earthenware 121-2, *121*, *123*
Eastlake chairs *17*
Edgell, Simon 79
Egyptian revival *25*
Ellis, Joel 153
Elmslie, George Grant 57
Empire style 29, 31, 34
  beds 34
  chairs 12
  sofas 17
  tables 25
enameling
  glass 94, *109*, *116*
  silver *75*
Eustis, Ebenezer *33*
Eyck, Koenraet Ten 68

F
faience *131*, 132
fakes
  banjo clocks 63
Federal style
  chairs 11-12, *14*, *15*, *20*
  clocks *60*
  mirrors 42
  pewter 81
  secretaries 31, *33*
  silver 69, 71
  tables *24*, 25, *25*
feet
  animal 17, 25
  ball 11, 26, 34
  bracket *10*, 31
  claw-and-ball 11, 17, 22, 28, 34, *86*
  club 11
  Dutch 22
  French 29, 31
  hairy paw 11
  pad 11, 17, 22, 34
  paw 25
  reeded 29
  scroll 11, 29
  slipper 22
  Spanish 11, 22, 34
  trifid 11, 22
  webbed 22
Fenton, Christopher Webber 125
fielded panels *10*
figureheads 159-60
Filley, Oliver 87
firearms 166-71
  flintlock 167, *167*, 170
  muskets 167
  percussion cap 167
  pistols 167
  revolvers *167*, *168*, 170-1, *171*
  rifles 167, 170, *170*, 171
First American Doll Factory 153
Fisher Brothers 99
floorcloths 144
Folwell, John 28
Fostoria Glass 118
French Antique style 29
Frost, Edward Sands 147
Fry, Laura A. 132
Fry Glass Company 118
Fueter, Daniel Christian 71
furniture
  caned, 11, 17, *17*, 18, 33
  casters 25
  gilding 25, *41*, 42, *42*, *62*, *63*
  inlaid decoration 24, 25, 28
  japanned 26, 28, 41
  laminated 15, 18, *19*
  mass-produced 15
  metalwork *56*
  painted and decorative finishes *see* PAINTED AND DECORATIVE FINISHES
  papier-mâché 42
  stenciled decoration *14*, 15
  upholstered 17-20
  veneers *26*, 29, 41
  verre eglomisé technique 33, 42

G
Gaines, John *11*
Gallatin, Albert, Glass Works 99
Garcia, Father 165
Ghiselin, Cesar 70
gilding *41*, 42, *42*, *62*, *63*
  ceramics 129
  furniture and clocks 25, *41*, 42, *42*, *62*, *63*
  glass 94, *116*
glass 90-119
  banjo clocks 63, *63*
  blown-molded *107*, *108*
  carnival 109
  cut 100, *111*
  enameled 94, 98, *109*, *116*
  flint-glass (lead glass) 98, 99
  free-blown 91, *91*, *92*, *93*, 94, *94*, *95*, *96*, *97*
  gilding, 94, *116*
  lacy patterns 105, 109
  leaded *115*
  machine-pressed 104-5, *106*, *108*, 109
  mass-produced 109
  milk 109
  mirrors *see* MIRRORS
  mold-blown glass 100, *104*
  pattern-molded 94, *96*, 98-100, *98*, 100, *101*
  pictorial and commemorative 100, *102*, 103-4, *103*, *104*, *105*
  pressed 99
  South Jersey 91
  tableware 91
  Tiffany 58
  verre eglomisé 33, 42
Glass House Company 91
Glassboro Works 91
Gleason, William, & Sons 159
Goddard, John *21*, 30
goldsmiths 67
Gorham & Company 72, 75
Gostelowe, Jonathan 28
Gothic Revival 33
Graves, Richard 79
Greek Revival 29, 34
Greene, Charles Sumner *56*, *57*, 58, *58*, 130
Greene, Henry Mather *56*, *57*, 58, *58*, 130
Greiner, Ludwig 153, *155*
Grueby Faience and Tile Company *131*

H
Harland, Thomas 61
Harmony Glassworks 91
Harrison, John 125
Harvard Monteith 69
harvest jug *121*
Hastings & Gleaston 159
Hawken Brothers 170
Hemphill, Alexander 129
Hemphill, Joseph *129*
Henchman, Daniel 72
Henderson, David 125
Hepplewhite style
  chairs 12, *15*
  chests of drawers 29
  tables 24, 25
Herter, Gustave 75
Herter Brothers 58
highboys 26, 28-9, *28*, 30
  Van Pelt highboy 29
historical items
  ceramics 125, 126
  figureheads and shop signs 159, 160
  glass 100, *102*, 103-4, *103*, *104*, *105*
Hitchcock, Lambert *14*, 15, 64
Hobbs, Brockunier and Company *117*
Hoffman, Solomon 153
Holl, Peter *43*
Horsman, E.I., Company 153-4
Hotchkiss, Arthur E. *157*
Hubbard, Elbert 58
Hudson, Ira 162
Hulbeart, Philip 71
Hull, John 67, 68
Hulme, John 129
Humphreys, Richard 71
Hurd, Benjamin 71
Hurd, Jacob 71, *73*
Hurd, Nathaniel 71

I
Imperial Glass Company 118
Indiana Tumbler and Goblet Company 106
inkstand *79*
International Silver Company 77
ironwork 81, 83, 85

toys 156
Isabella Glass Works *103*
Ives, Edward R. 157
Ives, Joseph *62*
Ives and Blakeslee *157*

J
'Jacobean' style 11, 17, 21
japanning
furniture 26, 28, 41
toleware 85-6, *86, 87*
Jarves, Deming 104, 111
Jenny, Burnham & Root 57
Jerome Brothers 64
Jersey Porcelain & Earthenware Company 129
jewelry, Navajo and Indian 7, *78,* 87-9, *88, 89*

K
K & K Toy Company 155
Kentucky rifle 167, 170, *170*
kettles 83
Kierstede, Cornelius 68
Kimble Glass 111
Kip, Jesse 68
Kirk, Samuel, & Sons 77
Knickerbocker Toy Company 154
Knowles, Taylor & Knowles 130

L
lacquered (japanned) furniture 26, 28, 41
Laing, Albert 162
Lancaster Valley rifle 167
Lannuier, Charles-Honoré 12
Ledel, Joseph 70
Lee, Michael 79
Lefferts, M.C. 153
legs
ball-and-cone 28
cabriole 11, *11,* 17, 22, 28
fluted 17
inverted-cup 28
lyre supports 25
sabre 12
tripod 22
Lenox, Walter 130
LeRoux, Bartholomew 68
Lewis and Clark 167, 170
Libbey Glass 111, 112
Lincoln, Joe 162
Locke, Joseph 111
Lockport glassworks 104
Long, William A. 132
Lonhuda Pottery 132
'Louis XVI' style 15
lounge 17
Louwelsa Pottery 132
love-seat *19*
Low, John G. 132
lowboys 28, *29, 30*
Lyman & Fenton 129
lyre supports 25

M
McIntire, Samuel *25,* 29, 159
McLaughlin, Mary Louise 130
Maher, George Washington 57
Mallard, Prudent 36
Mansfield, John 67
Mary Pease chest 39
Mason Decoy Factory 162
mass-production
clocks 62, 63, 64
decoy ducks 162
furniture 15
glass 109
shop signs 160
Melchers, Julius Theodore 160
Meriden Brittania Company 77
metalwork 78-89
furniture *56*
japanned (toleware) 85-6, *86, 87*
silver 66-77
toys 151, 156-7, *156*
Milford glass *96*
Minott, Samuel 71
mirrors 41-3
architectural style 4?
candle arm *40*
chimney 42
convex *40,* 42
mirror clocks *62*
overmantel *41,* 42
painted *40*
pier 42
sconces 42
missal stand *52*
Mission furniture 58
monteiths 69, 71, *72*
Montgomery Ward 147
Moore, Edward C. 75, *75*
Moravian sect 122
Morgan, Matt, Art Pottery 130
Morris, George Anthony 129
Mount Washington Glassworks 111-12, *116, 117*
mourning pictures 137
mugs, silver 69-70
music boxes 157
Myers, Myer 71, *73*

N
Nash, A. Douglas, Co. 111
Navajo and Indian Jewelry 7, *78,* 87-9, *88, 89*
needlework *see* QUILTS AND COVERLETS; RUGS; TEXTILES
neo-Baroque style 29
neo-Gothic style 29
New Bremen Glass *93,* 94, *95, 96*
New England Glass Company 99, 105, 111, *117*
New Geneva Glass Works *100*
New York tankard 70
Newton, Clara Chapman 132
Nichols, Maria Longworth 130, 132
Noah's Arks 149
Norton, Captain John 125
Norton, Julius 125
Norton & Fenton 129
Nys, Johannis 70

O
ormolu clock *64*
Osgood, Captain 162
Ott & Brewer 130
Owens, J.B., Pottery 132

P
painted and decorative finishes
clocks *61*
furniture 36, *26,* 44-5, *45*
gilding *41,* 42, *42, 62, 63,* 94, *116,* 129
inlay 58
japanning 26, 28, 41, 85-7, *86, 87*
mirror frames *40,* 41, *41,* 42
Pennsylvania Dutch furniture 44-5, *45*
simulated tortoiseshell 41
Southwestern style 49, 51, *52,* 56
stenciling *see* STENCILED DECORATION
toleware 85-7, *86, 87*
Pairpoint, Thomas J. 72
papier-mâché
clocks 64
dolls *154*
furniture 42, 87
Parian ware 129, *129*
Pattison, Edward 86
Pattison, William 86
Pendleton Glass Works *103*
Pennsylvania Dutch
beds 45
ceramics 122, *122, 123*
chairs 45
furniture 43-5, *43, 45,* 49
metalware 85
toys 149, *149, 150,* 151
Pennsylvania rifle 167
Pereyro, Father 165
pewter 79, *79,* 81
Philadelphia Glass Works 98-9
Philadelphia Tin Toy Manufactory 156
Phyfe, Duncan 12, *12, 14, 17,* 17, *18,* 25
Pietist sect 122
Pittsburgh Flint Glass Manufacturing Company 104, 105
Pittsburgh Glass Works 99
Plains rifle 170
porcelain 126-7, 126, 127, 128, 129-30, *129*
clocks 64
dolls 153
porringers *66, 68,* 68-9, 70
Prairie School 56-7
press cupboards 39, 41
Purcell and Elmslie *59*
Putnam, Grace Storey 155

Q
'Queen Anne' style 34, *36, 40,* 41
beds 34
chairs 11, *11, 14,* 17
desks 30, *31*
highboys *26,* 28
mirrors *40,* 41
silver 69
tables 22
Quezal Art Glass 111
Quezel Decorating Company *115*
quilts and coverlets 137-9, *138, 139, 140, 141, 142, 143,* 144, *144, 145,* 147
couch-quilted 137
Linsey-woolseys 138
patchwork 137, 138-9, 144
trapunto 137, *137*

R
railways, model 157
Randolph, Benjamin 11
Rank, Johannes *45*
Rasch, Anthony *71*
Redford Crown Glass Works *94*
redware 121, *121*
Reed & Barton 77, 81
'Regency' style *see* EMPIRE STYLE
Remington, Eliphalet, Jr. 171
Remington, Frederick 7
Remington firearms, *166, 167, 168,* 171
Renaissance Revival *13,* 33, 34, 36, 75
retablos 165
Revere, Paul, Jr 71, 72
Revere, T. *69*
Rich, Gideon 61
Richardson, Francis 70
Richardson, Henry Hobson 57
Richardson, Joseph 70, *70,* 71
Richardson, Joseph, Jr 72
Rittenhouse, David 61, *62*
Rivoire, Apollos 71
Robb, Samuel A. 160
Roberts, John 61
rocking horses 151
Rockwood pottery *132*
Rockwood Standard pottery *124*
Rococo Revival 18, *19,* 34, 36
Rococo style 30, 70-1
Rockwood Pottery 7, 58, 130, *130,* 132, *133*
Root, Elisha K. 171
Roseville Art Pottery 132
Roseville Pottery Co. *133*
Ross, Ebenezer 147
Roycrofters 58
rugs
braided 144, *146*
drawn-in *146*

hooked 144, *146*
knitted *147*
shirred 144
throws 144
Rush, William 159
rush-seated chairs 11, 15

S
samplers *134*, 135, *135*, *136*, 137
Sanderson, Robert 67
Sandwich Glass Company *105*, *114*
santos 162, *164*, 165
sauceboat *71*
Savannah pottery 127
Savery, William 28
Schank, Gerrit 72
schranks *43*, 45
Scott, Isaac E. 58
secretaries 30, 31, *32*
settees 17
settle *56*
Seymour, John *23*
Seymour, Thomas *23*
sgraffito decoration 122, *122*, *123*
Shaker furniture 45-9, *45*, *46*, *47*, *48*
Sheraton style
beds 34
chairs 12, *12*, *14*, *20*
chests of drawers 29
desks 33
secretaries 31
sofas 12
tables 24, 25
Shirayamadani, Kuitaro 132
shop signs *158*, 160
Sicard, Jacques 132
Silsbee, J.L. 57
silver 66-77
Singer, Thomas *89*
slipware *120*, 122, *124*, *125*
Smith, Horace 171
Smith & Wesson 171
snuff box *70*
sofas 12, 17-18, *17*, *18*, *19*, *21*, 34
Sons of Liberty Bowl 72
Soumain, Simeon 73
South Jersey glass 91
Southwark, Philadelphia, chinaworks 127, 129
Southwestern style 49-51, *49*, 51, *52*, 56
Spanish-Mexican style *see* SOUTHWESTERN STYLE
Spiegel, Jacobus van der 70
spring-action toys 156-7
Stanger, Jacob 91
stenciled decoration *151*
ceramics 122
clocks 64, *64*
furniture *14*, 15
toleware 87
sternboards 159-60
Steuben Glass Company *96*, *110*, 111, *111*, 118, *118*
Stevens, J. & E. 156, 157
Stickley, Gustave *56*, 58, *58*
Stiegel, William 'Baron' 94
stoneware 122, *124*
stools 11
Storer, Richard 67
sugar boxes 69
Sullivan, Louis H. 57
Syng, Philip, Jr. 70

T
tables 21-4
bird-cage mechanism 22
breakfast 22
butterfly 21
candlestands 22, *24*
card *21*, 22, *25*
dining 22, *22*, *24*, 25
drop-leaf 22, 24
drum *23*
Dutch tray 22
extension 24
gaming 24
gateleg 21, 22
lyre supports 25
mixing *24*
pedestal 24, 25
Pembroke 22, *23*
pie-crust edge 22
pier 25, 42
refectory-style 21
shell-and-scroll edge 22
sofa 25
tavern (taproom) 21, 22
tea 22, *26*
tip-and turn 22, *26*
tray top 22, *24*
trestle 21, *22*
tankards *68*, 69, 69-70
Taylor, William Watts 132
tea caddies (canisters) 74, *122*
teapots and services
silver 70, 73-5, *73*, *74*, *75*
tinware 85
Terry, Eli 62, 63, 64, *64*
textiles 134-47
pictorial panels 137
samplers *134*, 135, *135*, *136*, 137
turkey-work 11, 17
see also QUILTS AND COVERLETS; RUGS
Thiekson, Joseph 122
Thomas, Seth, Clock Co. *63*
Thomson, William *71*
Thonet, Michael 15
Tiffany, Charles Louis 75, 111
Tiffany, Louis Comfort 7, 75, 77, 111, 117, *117*, *119*
Tiffany & Company 111
clocks *61*, *64*
silver 72, 75, *75*, *76*, 76, 77, *77*
Tiffany Glass and Decorating Company 58, *77*, 111, *113*, *115*, 117, *117*, *119*
tin toys 151, 156-7, *156*
tinware 45, 81, 83, *83*, *84*
Tobey Furniture Company 58
toleware 85-7, *86*, *87*
tortoiseshell, simulated 41
Tower Toy Company (Tower Guild) 151
Townsend, John *23*, *29*
Townsend-Goddard family (cabinet makers) 28, 30
toy soldiers *148*
toys 148-57
trapunto 137, *137*
trasero 51, *52*, 56
Tucker, William Ellis 129, *129*
Tucker & Hemphill 129
Tucker & Hulme 129
Tufft, Thomas *14*, 28
tureen *71*
turkey-work 11, 17

U
Umland, Johann *33*, *34*
Union Glass Company 111, *112*, 117
Union Porcelain Works 129
United States Pottery Co. 129
upholstery 11, 17-20

V
Valentine, Albert R. 132
Van Briggle, Artus 132
Van der Burgh, Cornelius 68, 69
Van Dyck, Peter 68, 70
Van Inbrugh, Peter 68, 70
Van Pelt highboy 29
Van Voorhis, Daniel 72
veneers 26, *26*, 29, 41
verre eglomisé 33, 42
Vilant, William 70
Vineland Flint Glass Works 111

W
wag-on-the-wall 62, 63
Walker, Captain Samuel 170
Walker, Mrs. Izannah 154
weathervanes *79*, *80*, 81, *81*, *82*, 83
Wesson, Daniel 171
West, Robert *21*
Weston, William Henry 162
Wheatley, T.J., Pottery 130
Wheeler, Captain Artemas 170
Wheeler, Charles 'Shang' 7, 162
Whiting Manufacturing Company 77
Whitney Glass Works *104*
Wilkinson, George 72
Will, Henry 79, *79*
Will, William 79
Willard family (clockmakers) 61-2, 63, 64
William Cullen Bryant Vase 72
'William and Mary' style *36*, 41
beds 34
chairs 11, *11*, 11, *11*
desks *29*, 30
lowboys 28
mirrors 41
silver 69
tables 11, 21-2
Winchester rifle 171
Winchester-Hotchkiss rifle *170*
Windsor chairs and settees 11, *12*, 17
Wistar, Caspar 91
Wistarburg glasshouse 91
Wood & Hughes 77
wood-carving *6*, 158-65, *158*, *159*, *160*, *161*, *162*, *163*, *164*, *165*
Arts and Crafts movement 56
chip-carving 36, *52*
Frisian chip-carving 36
Southwestern style 51, *51*
wooden toys *148*, 149, *149*, *150*, 151-2, *151*, 153
woods
ash 11, 26
birch 12, 15
bird's-eye maple *23*
black walnut 18
burl veneers 26, *26*, 30
cherry *24*, 30, 34
cottonwood 51
fall front 30
flame birch *23*
fruitwood 21, 36
inlaid 24, 25
juniper 51
mahogany 11, 12, *15*, *17*, *20* *21*, 22, *23*, 25, 27, 28, 30, 31, 34, *35*, *40*, 42, 61
maple 11, 12, 15, 21, 26, 28, 30, 31, 33, 34, *37*, 167
mesquite 51
oak 21, 26, 30, 33, 36, *37*, 38, *56*
pine *15*, 21, 26, 30, 33, 36, *37*, 51
poplar *15*
rosewood 12, 18, *19*, 25, 34, *36*
satinwood 12, *15*
teak *56*
veneers 26, *26*, 29, 41
walnut 11, 21, 22, 26, *26*, 28, 30, *30*, 167
wool-on-wool coverlets 137
Wooton's Patent desk *31*, *32*
Wright, Frank Lloyd *56*, 57, *57*
writing boxes 29, 36

Y
Yale, Hiram 81
Young, Grace *124*
Young, Peter 79
Youngs, Benjamin *46*

Z
Zuni Indiand 89